Breakthrough
to the Computer Age

Breakthrough to the Computer Age

HARRY WULFORST

CHARLES SCRIBNER'S SONS
NEW YORK

To Marjorie

Copyright © 1982 Harry Wulforst

Library of Congress Cataloging in Publication Data

Wulforst, Harry.

Breakthrough to the computer age.
Bibliography: p.
Includes index.
1. Computers—History. I. Title.
QA76.17.W84   001.64′09   82-842
ISBN 0-684-17499-5   AACR2

1 3 5 7 9 11 13 15 17 19   F/C   20 18 16 14 12 10 8 6 4 2

Printed in the United States of America.

Contents

Acknowledgments

This book could not have been written without the valued commentaries and personal reminiscences of more than thirty scientists and engineers who participated in the development of the world's first electronic computers.

A special debt of gratitude is owed to Dr. Christopher Evans, who, in association with the Science Museum of London, tape recorded interviews of many computer pioneers in Great Britain and Europe. A similar debt is owed to Dr. Uta C. Merzbach, who graciously granted access to the voluminous store of computer history transcripts at the Smithsonian Institution.

I am also indebted to Juanita G. Gordon of General Instrument Corporation and to Clement G. Vitek of the *Baltimore Sun,* who provided vital background information used in chapters 10, 11, and 13. And finally, my thanks to William Grover, Sheldon Kapustin, and Philip S. Vincent, whose massive files of memoranda, letters, and reports on ENIAC, BINAC, and UNIVAC I were indispensable in documenting the sequence of events.

Introduction

It was an unlikely beginning.
A memorandum, filed and forgotten.
An idea, discredited and rejected.
A simple wire circuit, the only tangible evidence to back an incredible proposal: Build a huge electronic calculator and in minutes it will spew out more data than scores of mathematicians can produce in months.

On a gray and windy morning in March 1943, a young army officer bounded up a staircase in the University of Pennsylvania's Moore School of Electrical Engineering, seeking a man who might know how to resolve his dilemma. Six months earlier, Lieut. Herman H. Goldstine had come to Philadelphia to oversee a cadre of civilians working on ballistics problems for the Proving Ground in Aberdeen, Maryland. The solutions to those problems would eventually save precious time in combat. Just a slight change in wind direction, a drop in temperature, or even a switch to another type of ammunition can draw a well-

1

sighted gun off target. When this happens, a glance at firing tables, sometimes bound in a handy little book, enables a gun commander to find the new and correct angle of elevation quickly and to resume firing.

Now that America's war industries were moving into high gear, more large guns were rolling off production lines. But completing the firing tables for them required a staggering number of long calculations, and the army's main computation center at Aberdeen and the substation in the Moore School were hard pressed to keep pace. There was also mounting concern that there might not be enough qualified people around to do the computing for the additional armament to be produced later in the war. Clearly, something had to be done to erase the specter of huge guns stored and silent in depots because no one had supplied the data to aim and fire them. Goldstine's mission was to help prevent this from happening and to accelerate the work of the computers, as they were called, in the Moore School contingent. But there were limits. Goldstine knew that calculations could not be hurried at the expense of accuracy. Yet, if output did not increase, he feared that his unit would never be able to satisfy the growing demand for more firing tables.

Then came the discovery, quite by chance, that a professor at the Moore School had been trying to sell a bizarre, but intriguing, idea: A machine without moving parts (an electronic computer, he said) could easily surpass the combined outputs of thousands of mechanical calculators. The man whom Goldstine sought that morning was John W. Mauchly, a thirty-six-year-old physicist. When Goldstine found him, the means to prevent a firing table crisis seemed within reach. A prospect that had been bleak had unexpectedly brightened.

For centuries, man's ability to probe the mysteries of the physical universe was limited by the lack of appropriate tools. Blaise Pascal's Arithmetic Machine, conceived in 1642; Baron Gottfried Wilhelm von Leibniz's calculator, completed in 1694, which performed all four operations of arithmetic; and Charles Babbage's Difference Engine, which he began building in 1822, were significant accomplishments in their time. But they did not lighten, in any measurable way, the onerous burden of calculating by hand. Babbage's Difference Engine, for example, and his later, more complex Analytical Engine remained unfinished when he died in 1871.

Meanwhile, calculations and paperwork mushroomed in business and government throughout the nineteenth century. Clerks by the thousands, working day and night, barely kept up with the growing volume. For example, the situation steadily worsened at the United States Bureau of the Census. Since 1800 each succeeding decennial count took more time to process than the previous one. It took nearly seven years to compile the data gathered in the census of 1880, and when finally published, the information was obsolete and practically useless. Census officials desperately sought ways to prevent the bureau from foundering in the sea of paper that threatened to engulf it in 1890. A young statistician named Herman Hollerith proposed a method that looked promising. If data received from census takers was punched in cards, said Hollerith, then the coded patterns of holes could be sensed and read not once but many times. There would be no need to rerecord the same data for similar calculations that might be needed weeks or months in the future. By merely rerunning the cards through an electric tabulator, many of the earlier repetitious and time-consuming hand calculations would be eliminated. After exhaustive tests Hollerith's punched-card system was adopted and put to work processing the 1890 census.

The results were astonishing. Not only was more data processed than ever before, but the job was finished in one-fourth the time needed to compute the 1880 census. Of more lasting significance was the fact that the new punched-card technique made it possible to analyze the base information in ways that could never be attempted manually. Hollerith's success attracted considerable attention, and it soon became apparent that the electric tabulator offered benefits and capabilities that extended far beyond computing census data. Almost overnight there was a budding new market for such machines. To develop his invention, Hollerith formed a company that years later and after a series of acquisitions and mergers would become International Business Machines Corporation (IBM). Around the turn of the century, James Powers, an associate of Hollerith also formed a company to manufacture, market, and service mechanical tabulating equipment. In 1927 the Powers Company, along with several other business machine manufacturers, became the nucleus for the data-processing operations of Remington Rand, which later, in 1955, would merge with Sperry Corporation.

By 1940 punched-card data processing was firmly entrenched in business and government. Every day tens of thousands of mechanical sorters, collators, and tabulators whirred and chewed their way through the steadily rising torrent of paperwork. But gears, cams, and pinions can only turn so fast, and once their limit is reached, there is no way to increase the amount of work they can do. While in 1890 Hollerith's machine broke through the barrier, over the years his once revolutionary punched-card techniques had been honed and refined so much that by 1940 each newly designed machine seemed to be a tiny step and not a giant leap forward.

For the businessman the ceiling on processing speed was a bother and an expense. If one tabulator could not do the day's work, he bought another, and then another. For the scientist and the mathematician, the ceiling meant frustration and disappointment. While punched-card data-processing techniques offered a tantalizing glimpse of what might be learned with machines a thousand times faster, the limits imposed by mechanical principles dispelled such thoughts from the start.

The first hint of relief surfaced in 1943. Only a lieutenant and hardly in a position to influence the upper echelons of the War Department, Goldstine nevertheless argued vigorously in support of Mauchly's proposal. Paul N. Gillon, then a major in the Ballistic Research Laboratory at Aberdeen, was won over and cleared the way for a review of the idea by a technical commission composed of eminent scientists and high-ranking army officers. Spearheaded by the enthusiasm of Gillon and Goldstine, the proposal was quickly approved and an initial grant of $61,700 was awarded to the University of Pennsylvania to start building an electronic computer.

While Mauchly and his collaborator, J. Presper Eckert, Jr., worked in a converted classroom, military secrecy shrouded what was going on there for almost three years. False stories were leaked alleging that the locked and guarded room on the first floor of the Moore School housed a machine that had turned out to be a "white elephant." Project PX, however, was by no means a failure. On February 15, 1946, a front-page story in the *New York Times* described the unprecedented power and speed of ENIAC— an electronic calculator that performed as many as 5,000 additions in one second.

For scientists the unveiling of ENIAC was as electrifying as the discovery of gold in California had been to fortune hunters nearly a century earlier. In quick succession scores of electronic computer projects were started in the United States, England, Europe, Scandinavia, Australia, and Japan. By 1955 the issue was no longer in doubt: There had been a breakthrough of staggering proportions.

A few dedicated men and women, virtually unknown outside their own professional circles, had launched a new era. In less than three decades their pioneering would, among other things, revolutionize business practices, make it possible for man to rocket to the moon and return, create a new multibillion dollar computer industry, and positively or adversely influence the lives (the debate still goes on) of nearly every human being in the civilized world.

This is the story of that breakthrough.

CHAPTER 1

The Firing Table Crisis

The Allied noose tightened around Bizerte, Tunisia, in the spring of 1943. In the months since the beachheads were won in Morocco and Algeria in November 1942, more than a half-million square miles of enemy-controlled territory had been liberated. The Afrika Korps, once the scourge of the continent, was on the verge of collapse. The home front in America, buoyed by dispatches from the front, awaited the first unconditional surrender of Axis forces to the Allied army. The North African campaign, however, had been long and bitterly contested.

The first setback came shortly after the landings on November 8, 1942. Record Tunisian winter rains thwarted a quick thrust eastward, and Gen. Dwight D. Eisenhower's columns stalled short of their objectives. The delay gave Germany and Italy time to shuttle fresh troops from Sicily. Heavily reinforced, the Axis forces dug in while the Allies reformed their lines in the freezing Tunisian hills. In mid-January Eisenhower decided to concentrate on building up his forces, delaying a renewed offensive until spring. In the interim, the Germans exploited their advantage. While Allied planes remained bogged down on muddy Tunisian air fields, the Luftwaffe operated freely from hard-topped bases around Tunis. Frequent armored thrusts into Allied lines, continual harassment from the air, a costly reverse at the Kasserine Pass, and the stiff resistance encountered at Hill 609 complicated the Allied advance. But by May 13, 1943, the Axis grip on North Africa was broken. More than 250,000 German and Italian troops had been herded into prison compounds, and the Allies could then get on with the invasions of Sicily and Italy.

The lessons learned in North Africa were the kind only learned in battle. Armed conflict, after all, is the ultimate test of men and materiel. The North African campaign answered questions, identified weaknesses, and corroborated strengths with clarity and finality. Ranked high in the record of military accomplishments during the campaign was the experience gained with modern weapons and equipment. Much of the intelligence relating to weaponry that came from North Africa was directed to the Proving Ground in Aberdeen, Maryland. At Aberdeen, a vast restricted area that stretches along the shore of the Chesapeake Bay for almost thirty-five miles, all types of armament were tested before acceptance by the military. In addition to managing the operation of its many firing ranges, the Aberdeen staff also devised improvements for existing weapons, developed ideas for new ones, and generated reams of ballistics data for the use and care of ordnance in the field.

Before World War I, only thirty years earlier, not much was known about ballistics. Until then, most of the gains were based on the work of Francis Bashforth, an Englishman. Around 1850 he devised a way to relate drag (the slowing force that the atmosphere exerts on any body moving through it) to velocity. Using Bashforth's ideas, ballisticians finally began to compute some relevant data on the drag function. In the last two decades of the nineteenth century, a commission working in Gavré, France, further organized and refined the data into what became known as the Gavré Function. This was applied extensively during World War I to determine the ballistics characteristics of nearly all sizes of shells, even though it was a bad-to-poor approximation for many of them.

The difficulties spawned by the wholesale use of the Gavré Function were compounded by another questionable practice. A vast amount of the numerical work required to calculate trajectories could be bypassed by upgrading arbitrary assumptions to the level of established fact. One common assumption, for example, held that the density of air remained constant with altitude. That myth exploded dramatically in the early part of World War I when startled German ordnance experts test-fired a powerful new naval gun and found its range to be twice the distance they had predicted. Most of the shell's trajectory was through air only half as dense as that at ground level. With less drag at the higher altitudes, it zoomed far beyond its intended target. The Germans quickly applied this discovery in the design of a new long-range gun, dubbed "Big Bertha," which they later fired against Paris.

Meanwhile, in America, sensing that the developing expertise in Europe called for an extraordinary response, the high command of the United States Army directed the Ordnance Corps to accelerate ballistics research. One group, in the ballistics branch of the Office of the Chief of Ordnance in Washington, D.C., was under the leadership of Forest Ray Moulton. Another group, headed by Oswald Veblen, a former professor at Princeton, was formed at Sandy Hook, New Jersey. (A very junior member of the Sandy Hook team, a young private named Norbert Wiener, would gain international recognition some thirty years later for his pioneering work in cybernetics and his book *The Human Use of Human Beings*.) Neither Moulton, a distinguished astronomer, nor Veblen, a noted mathematician, seemed to fit the stereotype of an academic. Even though they had pursued parallel careers at the University of Chicago, first as graduate students, then as members of the faculty, and both were scientists of the first magnitude, they possessed attributes rarely found in a university environment—they were superb administrators and managers of people.

Moulton and Veblen expertly fulfilled their missions during World War I and went on to ensure a high standing for the United States in ballistics research throughout the 1920s and 1930s. Moulton, for instance, managed to persuade the War and Navy departments to begin sending their most promising young officers to the University of Chicago to undertake advanced graduate studies in mathematics. This assured a continuing supply of mathematical expertise to the army's ordnance branch and its ballistic research work at the Aberdeen Proving Ground. Also, by creating career paths for civilian employees, the negative effects of rotating senior officers through different commands were largely neutralized. Samuel Feltman, for example, a civilian employee who had done hand calculating during World War I for the ordnance department, rose to become the equivalent of the permanent underchief of ballistics work in Washington. For many years, while serving under a series of officers, most of whom had little technical training, Feltman managed to provide the continuity and the stability to keep the important long-range objectives on target. Similarly, another civilian, Robert H. Kent, had been teaching electrical engineering at the University of Pennsylvania in 1917. With America's entry into the war, he volunteered, was commissioned a lieutenant of ordnance, and went to work in Moulton's office in Washington. Two years later, after reaching the rank of captain following service in France, he was discharged and rejoined the Washington office as a civilian. In 1922 he transferred to the Ballistic

Research Laboratory, where he remained throughout a long and distinguished career.

While a future for ballistics research seemed assured, prospects for substantive progress were less certain. To move ahead, new ways had to be found to crunch and digest massive columns of numbers. The crux of the problem was the differential equation. Although dynamic physical situations could be described mathematically in differential equations, no one had yet built the apparatus that could cope with the volume of calculations needed to thoroughly analyze those descriptions. Of course, some differential equations can be solved unaided; most, however, are sufficiently complex to make it difficult, if not impossible, to hand calculate more than a single specific solution in any acceptable time frame. For ballisticians, who were not so much interested in a single solution as they were in whole families of solutions, it was an impasse of massive proportions. The need was by no means limited to ballistics research. The lack of adequate tools was also slowing down work in such centers of advanced technology as Bell Telephone Laboratories, General Electric Company, and the Massachusetts Institute of Technology.

One of the more serious trouble spots was electric power. As incandescent lamps, refrigerators, and other modern appliances boosted the consumption of electricity in the 1920s, new and perplexing problems kept cropping up. To begin with, getting sufficient energy to every factory, office, and household called for the design and construction of huge electric power stations and the erection of vast transmission networks. Generating and delivering the power was one thing, but properly balancing the supply and the demand, throughout hundreds of square miles of city and countryside, was something else. To achieve such a balance, engineers had to know how every element in the network would react to even slight changes in load. That kind of information could be developed only by thorough mathematical analyses, replete with differential equations. Although this was difficult enough, more complications arose when it became necessary to interconnect separate, though adjacent, power networks. Then the differential equations grew so complex that solving them was often beyond the combined capabilities of even the most talented engineers.

In a growing America, with the future supply of more electric power in jeopardy, finding a remedy rated high priority. Thousands of man-hours went into the search for a solution. In 1929 a device that its inventors called an A-C Network Analyzer was introduced jointly by the Massachusetts Institute of Technology and the General Electric Company. This cleverly conceived miniature power system could simulate, right in the laboratory, the behavior of large networks serving thousands of users via many miles of transmission lines. At last there was a tool that multiplied, by several orders of magnitude, an engineer's ability to solve differential equations. Yet, it was a special-purpose device. The help it provided was limited to a narrow field—generating and delivering electric power—and could not, in any way, ease the computational backlog inhibiting progress in other technologies. The network analyzer was a portent, nonetheless, of better things to come.

The fertile mind of Vannevar Bush, son of a Universalist minister and grandson of a Yankee whaling captain, would devise the general-purpose machine that everyone had been waiting for. Working with colleagues at the Massachusetts Institute of Technology, Bush directed the assembly of a bewildering array of wheels, gears, and shafts, and electric circuits, arranged at table-top height over an area approximately ten by thirty-five feet. In 1931 the Bush Differential Analyzer, then five years in the making, seemed to have all the earmarks of the ultimate mathematical robot. Very long and intricate differential equations, which scientists and mathematicians had previously called unsolvable, gradually succumbed to the methodical probing of Bush's new machine. Bush was quick to point out that these successes were by no means the upper limit. At the conclusion of a long description of the analyzer in the *Journal of the Franklin Institute* (October 1931), he wrote: "The machine is not yet completed. In fact, it is questionable that it ever will be ... for it can always be extended by adding more units to [solve more complex] equations."

Not surprisingly, the advent of the Differential Analyzer created quite a stir at Aberdeen. While there was much talk about building another one for ballistics research (Bush was willing to provide advice and counsel), no real progress was made for another two years. In the meantime, Bush had also been approached by representatives of the University of Pennsylvania who sought permission to build a copy for use in electrical engineering projects at the Moore School. In late 1933 a joint program was started by the army, the Moore School, and the Massachusetts Institute of Technology. To save time and effort, the same design approach was adopted by the ordnance department and the Moore School. The Aberdeen machine was built, under a War Department contract, by the Taft-Pierce Company, with Bush and colleagues from MIT supervising. The Moore School version was funded by the Civil Works Administration, one of the agencies created by President Franklin D. Roosevelt to stimulate the economy and provide some employment for skilled workers during the Depression of the 1930s. Both machines were completed in 1935 and were practically identical. Much earlier, the army, recognizing the value of a duplicate backup machine, had reached an agreement with the University of Pennsylvania whereby the Moore School installation would be made available for ballistics work in the event of a national emergency. The wisdom of that agreement would be demonstrated repeatedly only a few years later.

Before he turned fifty, Vannevar Bush had already earned

considerable recognition as an inventor and educator. But his early professional achievements, including his climb through the hierarchy of MIT to serve ultimately as vice president and dean of engineering, would later be almost eclipsed by his invaluable service to America at war. His sphere of influence had widened significantly in 1938 when he left MIT to become president of the Carnegie Institution in Washington, D.C. Set up by Andrew Carnegie in 1902, the institution had grown to be one of the world's largest scientific foundations. As president, Bush oversaw projects ranging from expeditions for the study of anthropology in Java to research in plant biology, embryology, genetics, nutrition, and terrestrial magnetism.

But his work outside the institution would be of far greater import. A firm believer that military preparedness was the best way to defend democracy in an age of dictatorships, Bush was alarmed by America's vulnerability as German armies swept across France and imperiled Britain. Although this was a worry shared by many scientists, it was Bush who seized the initiative. Shrewdly exploiting a friendship he had developed with Harry Hopkins, the close adviser to Franklin D. Roosevelt, Bush was granted an interview with the president in June 1940. He brought with him a plan of action, typed in four brief paragraphs on a single page. Ten minutes later he strode out of the Oval Office with the proposal in his hand, now inscribed with the brief inked notation: "OK—F.D.R." Roosevelt's imprimatur authorized the creation of a new independent agency, to be headed by Bush, called the National Defense Research Committee (NDRC). Its mission was to enlist "the support of scientific and educational institutions and organizations, and individual scientists and engineers throughout the country."

Bush wasted no time. He moved quickly to make the NDRC a highly visible and effective arm of the war effort. He was a brilliant protagonist. His forcefulness, tempered by wit, and an uncanny ability to disarm dissenters were known and respected throughout the highest echelons of government. Later, with characteristic modesty, he wrote in *Pieces of the Action:* "I made no technical contribution to the war effort. Not a single idea of mine ever amounted to shucks. . . . My job was to handle relations with the President, congress and the military services, and to try to keep the lines free and money available so that others could do some work."

While we may be persuaded to accept Bush's disclaimer that he made no technical contribution to the war effort when he headed NDRC, that certainly was not the case as far as his earlier work at MIT is concerned. Those who were in command at Aberdeen in the late 1930s and early 1940s are in agreement on this point: Without the Differential Analyzer, the Ballistic Research Laboratory could not have produced the record number of firing tables that were delivered to the fighting fronts during World War II.

Firing tables were indispensable to the artilleryman. By referring to them he could quickly make corrections for changes in air density, cross winds, temperature, and literally hundreds of other variables. In fact, for a gun the size of the 155mm "Long Tom," over 500 different conditions had to be dealt with, all of which were factored into firing tables. The basic information for computing these tables came from the test firings of artillery at Aberdeen. Instruments recorded muzzle velocities, recoil, point of impact, and scores of other readings that were eventually turned over to the Ballistic Research Laboratory for use in its computations. Firing tables for less sophisticated guns were sometimes printed in a book small enough to be carried in a pocket. For more advanced weapons equipped for radar input, target information could be fed directly into a robot-like device, preprogrammed with the appropriate firing tables, that positioned the piece automatically.

Compiling a set of firing tables was a long, arduous process. First, between 2,000 and 4,000 trajectories had to be plotted for every new gun design. Computing just one trajectory—the arcing flight path of a projectile from gun muzzle to impact—took a skilled operator using a desk calculator about twelve hours to complete. Bush's invention greatly speeded up this part of the process, but it was of no help later on. For after the trajectories were computed, there were many other computations that could not be delegated to the Differential Analyzer. Some of the most complex projects required as much as three additional months of work by scores of trained computers.

As war erupted in Europe, it became disturbingly clear that something had to be done to boost the output of firing tables by the Ballistic Research Laboratory. Paul Gillon, a captain at Aberdeen, was sent to Philadelphia to work out arrangements with Dean Harold Pender that would enable the army to take over the Moore School's Differential Analyzer. Around the same time, Gillon also started a training program at the Moore School to prepare new candidates for the overburdened staff at Aberdeen. With the military draft cutting into the supply of qualified males, Gillon organized recruitment appeals to women college graduates. He sent emissaries to scout the campuses of colleges and universities throughout the eastern United States. At first the emphasis was on seniors who had majored in mathematics, but when this pool of talent was exhausted, the requirements were relaxed in stages until late in the war, when liberal arts graduates with as little as two years of science were being recruited.

In July 1942, Herman H. Goldstine, a bright young mathematics professor at the University of Michigan was called into the army. During the late 1930s, while a junior member of the faculty at the University of Chicago, Goldstine had been an assistant to Gordon Bliss, a distinguished mathematician who had made important contributions to the mathematical theory of ballistics during World War I. Bliss wrote to Oswald Veblen, then the chief scientist of the Ballistic Research Laboratory, and recommended that Goldstine be attached to his staff. Veblen agreed and on August 7, 1942, Lieutenant Goldstine reported for duty at Aberdeen.

Soon after, Goldstine accompanied Gillon on an inspection trip of the Moore School. Years later Goldstine described the situation there: "We found things in a not very good state. . . . [The training program], like many other new projects, suffered from growing pains. Secondly, the faculty chosen by the University to teach mathematics consisted of several elderly professors emeriti who were no longer up to the strain of teaching day-long courses. Third, the cadre of trained people sent up from Aberdeen to run the Differential Analyzer and to do the other things needed to prepare firing tables was in need of leadership."

In September 1942 Goldstine was placed in charge of the entire operation in Philadelphia. While he went about pulling things together at the Moore School, some disquieting intelligence began filtering back from North Africa. Neither the soil (which influences recoil of a gun and subsequent behavior of a shell in flight) nor the climate in Algeria and Tunisia was a close fit for the environment in Aberdeen. But Aberdeen was where test-firing data had been compiled for subsequent use in ballistic computations. As a result, the firing tables for many of the army's guns in North Africa were slightly off kilter, and hitting a target was more difficult than it should have been. Here was another new and unexpected computation job for the overburdened Ballistic Research Laboratory. An aura of urgency and crisis settled over Aberdeen.

CHAPTER 2

In Search of a Number Cruncher

By 1943 the military maxims that had governed the conduct of war for centuries had been blasted beyond recall by the Blitzkrieg and the heavy bomber. The common soldier was now a technician as well as a combatant. No longer could a superior force, even one skillfully commanded and having an overwhelming tactical advantage, be assured of victory. By the imaginative use of technology, a small unit could repeatedly outwit and repel far stronger adversaries. Sir Robert Watson-Watt's timely invention of radar, for example, gave England's gallant but outnumbered fighter pilots the edge they needed to win the Battle of Britain. A redesigned bomb sight or a more responsive gun director may have been just as decisive as the impact of a fresh, well-trained division on a battle-weary enemy.

One of the ironies of the times was the fact that pure scientists—the very ones whose research had helped to bring about these changes—were looked upon as too theoretical to give any practical support to the war effort. While engineers and production specialists were being recruited en masse, no one seemed to know what to do about men with backgrounds as esoteric as that offered by John W. Mauchly.

In 1925, after winning a Maryland State scholarship, Mauchly entered Johns Hopkins University to major in engineering, but less than two years later, he was a disillusioned young man. He had found that engineers work only with principles that someone else had already defined. Mauchly didn't want that. As he later said, "It was cookbook stuff. You were told to design a girder to bear so much weight. All you did was look it up in a handbook—so many rivets, so big and where they went." More intrigued by the prospect of discovering principles than just applying them, he dropped engineering and switched to physics. But he couldn't decide whether he wanted to be a theoretical or an experimental physicist. Did he want to work in the laboratory or sit in a think tank and push a pencil around? He solved that problem by picking a field in which he could do both—molecular spectroscopy.

From Mauchly's viewpoint, molecular spectroscopy in the 1930s appeared to be the coming thing. Solving the mysteries of the molecules seemed to be just the kind of challenge he had been looking for. Moreover, it was a new field and the chances for making substantial headway were good. The tools were new, too. A basic one, the mass spectroscope, had been invented less than ten years earlier by Francis W. Aston.

Mauchly immersed himself in his new work. There was a lot to do, including learning how to shape and blow glass tubes, operate vacuum equipment, make high-voltage sparks, and sensitize and develop photographic plates. Years later Mauchly recalled: "I had to measure and interpret all of the lines in every plate. It was quite a job. Maybe twenty—or even thirty—thousand spectral lines would be generated by a single molecule." Afterward, to compute the results, he was faced with an interminably long series of calculations. For this part of the work, the only available tool was a small desk calculator. Students in his section called it the "lima bean machine" because its handle resembled a lima bean. During the years at Johns Hopkins, the lima bean machine would be his working partner for many thousands of hours.

Finally, in the spring of 1932, with his Ph.D. in hand, Mauchly thought that his days of cranking a calculator were behind him, but he soon found that a young physicist going out into a world racked by depression stood little chance of finding a job that had anything to do with his training. So Mauchly stayed at Johns Hopkins as a research assistant and earned enough to get by. For almost a year, he did many of the same things as before—measuring lines on photographic plates and computing the results on a calculator. This time, however, these tasks seemed more burdensome than ever. When he was a student, it had been his own research—now he was doing someone else's.

Then one day an opportunity for a better job materialized. Ursinus, a small private college about twenty-five miles west of Philadelphia, was looking for someone to head its physics department. Mauchly's friends at Johns Hopkins urged him to go after it. He did and after the post was offered to him, he learned that what most impressed the faculty were the names of his references. Letters of recommendation came from the pastor of his church, his high school principal, and from a man Mauchly hardly knew—John Campbell Merriam, then president of the prestigious Carnegie Institution. The ties with Dr. Merriam were more filial than professional. In 1914, when Mauchly was seven years old, his family moved from Cincinnati, Ohio, to a house in Chevy Chase, Maryland, that was within walking distance of the Carnegie Institution. His father, Herman E. Mauchly, had come to this suburb of Washington, D.C., to join Carnegie's Department of Terrestrial Magnetism as a staff physicist. The senior Mauchly died in 1928, but he is still remembered there as the man who discovered the "universal 24-hour term in the diurnal variation of the potential gradient of the earth's magnetic field."

Long before he entered Johns Hopkins, Mauchly had been a frequent visitor to his father's laboratory. Listening, watching, and sometimes lending a hand in an experiment, he had a front-row seat, so to speak, in what he considered the most fascinating theater on earth: a modern, well-equipped research facility. Soon after he started to learn his way around Carnegie, Mauchly felt that countless undiscovered treasures lay buried in its archives—the voluminous records of decades of scientific observations from all over the world. Hidden in those vast files were rare gems, random bits of evidence that, if properly pieced together, might dispel some of the mystery surrounding man's environment. A pipe dream? Perhaps. But Mauchly was sure that someday someone would pull it off. The trick was to find a way to plunge into that morass of records and then rapidly compress, digest, and analyze. The right tools for such a mammoth undertaking had not been invented, and the best calculators and punched-card equipment around could do little more than scratch the surface. Later, during his years at Johns Hopkins and summer recesses working as a lab assistant in the National Bureau of Standards, Mauchly persisted in the belief that one day a machine powerful enough to do such work would be built.

The professorship offered by Ursinus College, while a welcome change from the work at Johns Hopkins, would nonetheless inhibit Mauchly's progress in computing. Although justifiably proud of its new science building and the equipment acquired for an expanded physics program, Ursinus could not match the elaborate scientific paraphernalia to which Mauchly had become accustomed at Johns Hopkins. But he took the post, and, after a quick look at his new surroundings, Mauchly set out on a shopping tour of secondhand stores in Philadelphia and its environs. His objective was to buy the most useful general-purpose research tool that could be found, provided, of course, that it didn't exceed his department's "additional equipment" budget of $75.00. Eventually he found what he wanted, a used Marchant calculator, almost ten years old but apparently still in good condition. Sensing Mauchly's interest, the dealer hastened to close the sale. It was a good machine, he said, well taken care of and only one owner—a bank that had just been forced into receivership.

The sales pitch worked. Mauchly bought the calculator, and during most of his eight years at Ursinus, it was a handy thing to have around. Once in a while, however, he would be jolted by disturbing new evidence that it couldn't produce the volume of numbers he wanted. One day, for example, he decided to begin an ambitious new project—a detailed mathematical model of a complex molecule. Starting up took more time than he anticipated, and at the rate he was going, months of work during the day, after hours, and on weekends loomed ahead. Then, just a few weeks into the initial phase, he learned that a similar study was under way at Arthur D. Little Company, a large and reputable research organization in Cambridge, Massachusetts. A battery of punched-card machines there was churning out data for a mathematical model of a molecule 100 times faster than his hand calculator.

Clearly outclassed by this awesome display of computing power, Mauchly knew that it was futile to continue and compete, so he quietly shelved the project. At about the same time, his interest was again rekindled in the secrets that he believed lay hidden in the archives at Carnegie. If he didn't have those fancy punched-card machines to help him find them, maybe there were some other clever tricks he could use to ferret them out.

The science of statistics, he thought, might very well offer the kind of shortcuts he was looking for. After all, in recent years, statisticians had come up with a lot of new ways to collect, classify, analyze, and interpret data. Mauchly was also aware that, through the skilled application of mathematical theories of probability, order and regularity could be imposed on what appeared to be a random collection of unrelated numbers. Unfortunately, his background in this area was limited. As an undergraduate in Johns Hopkins, he had taken a course or two in conventional statistical mechanics, which was all that was required then for a student majoring in physics. His efforts to make up for this deficiency included the use of psychometrics— the measurement of mental traits and intellectual ability— in educational testing. Among other things, he and his colleagues were trying to analyze the relationship of a student's intelligence quotient to the grades he earned by applying advanced statistical techniques. While no great truths emerged from this study, the experience was nonetheless enlightening for Mauchly.

Throughout his tenure at Ursinus, he had kept in close touch with his friends at Johns Hopkins. In June 1936, with classes over and final grades posted, he was free to take a train down to Washington. But renewing old acquaintanceships wasn't the only reason for the trip. He also wanted to find out whether his new statistical skills could help him uncover ways to decipher and interpret the voluminous records compiled by Carnegie's Department of Terrestrial Magnetism. At first, his interest in those files had been inspired by the possibility of new discoveries in geophysics, but he later focused his sights on goals farther afield. From geophysical research, where findings were based on measurements of electric current in the atmosphere, it was a short and easy step to meteorology, the study of weather itself. Mauchly's interest in this subject was fueled by a debate between two factions in the geomagnetic community.

The argument was about sunspots. Did they or didn't they influence the weather? Most geophysicists staunchly maintained that there was no connection between solar activity and rainfall. Mauchly, who was considerably more open minded about this matter than many of his late father's associates, saw that those who were pushing the sunspot theory were at a serious disadvantage; because they had little training in statistics, the dubious "proofs" that they offered were easy to discredit and shoot down. If some way could be found to thoroughly analyze the government weather data at Carnegie, Mauchly was confident that cycles and patterns would come to light that would either corroborate or or disprove the sunspot theory once and for all.

By 1938 Mauchly's plan for a statistical assault on the Carnegie files was well under way. Two years earlier, during his summer visit to Washington, he had made arrangements to borrow parts of the records and take them back to Ursinus. But even though he had the records he wanted, Mauchly couldn't analyze them without help. To get that help, he persuaded the college registrar to bring his problem to the attention of the National Youth Administration (NYA), one of the numerous agencies created by the Roosevelt administration during the depression years.

The NYA had been paying students working part time fifty cents an hour for any task that fulfilled a worthwhile purpose. Until then, about the only NYA jobs available at Ursinus were cutting grass, raking leaves, stacking books, and pushing heavy rollers around the athletic field. For an agency with ample funds to pay students who wanted work, if only more work could be found, the Mauchly project was a bonanza. In short order, Mauchly had an authorization to organize a group of assistants. At first, he recruited only students who were majoring in mathematics, chemistry, or physics and put them to work sifting and copying the reams of meteorological data he had borrowed from Carnegie. If they could operate an adding machine and copy numbers accurately, they moved Mauchly a little closer to his goal. It really didn't matter that few of them understood what the number shuffling was all about.

Yet despite their help, progress was slow. As his student helpers pressed on, Mauchly kept hoping that new evidence would be found that would give him the leverage to ask for more funds. With more money, he could buy a punched-card machine and, he thought, speed up the process many times. But a visit to the New York World's Fair in the summer of 1939 would scotch that idea. On display at the fair were the most advanced punched-card systems in the world. As an obliging operator put each one through its paces, Mauchly made some quick calculations and was startled to find that even if he used as many as a dozen similar machines it still might take years to analyze the cartons of records that lay untouched in his laboratory storeroom.

In the months following this discovery, Mauchly began to think about leaving Ursinus. Hitler's legions had overrun Poland, Germany was at war with England and France, and America was being transformed into an "Arsenal of Democracy." Far out of the mainstream in a small country college, Mauchly felt that working in a defense plant would bring him closer to the action. However, the prospect of a higher salary and ready access to resources that might accelerate his work in computing were what really motivated him to begin searching for a new job. The quest would turn out to be a long one, for in industry Mauchly's eight years at Ursinus appeared to be a double handicap. First, his work had no counterpart in the war effort. Second, his prolonged association with the academic world, said one interviewer, rendered him unfit to cope with any practical assignment in industry. When he applied for a job in a company that employed a thousand chemists, Mauchly was told that they already had a physicist and didn't need a second one, especially not a college professor. Had he pursued the engineering career originally planned as a young man, Mauchly's job hunting might have been more fruitful.

Meanwhile, as he continued to search for a faster way to process the Carnegie files, an idea began to take shape in his mind. Several of the scientific journals to which he subscribed had been publishing reports about new measuring and counting techniques being applied in cosmic ray research. He was intrigued by the fact that the electronic circuits described in the articles could count many times faster than the combined speeds of a score or more punched-card machines. He hand wired some crude copies of the circuits to familiarize himself with the way they worked, and he then built more elaborate models, substituting gas tubes for conventional vacuum tubes, because the former needed less power and, being cheaper, were easier on his budget.

At the time, most apparatus used in cosmic ray research was electronic. The problem in that field had been to find a way to make a recorder (which barely counts 500 times a minute) keep pace with an electronic sensor that can detect thousands of events every second. One solution was to place a series of scaling circuits between the recorder and the sensor so that the cosmic ray counts could be cut down to a rate that the recorder could accept. Feeding two pulses into the first scaling circuit would produce a single output pulse. When this single pulse and a subsequent pulse entered a second circuit, the same thing happened again: two pulses in, one pulse out. Consequently, for one pulse to come out of the second scaling circuit, *four* pulses had to go into the first. And for a third scaling circuit in the line to produce one output pulse, eight separate inputs had to go into the first. If enough of these circuits were arranged in tandem, the slow mechanical recorder could keep track of cosmic ray bursts occurring thousands of times per second.

This was the kind of speed Mauchly had been looking for, but he knew that counting was a long way from computing. In order to compute, circuits had to perform basic arithmetic functions, make logical choices, and even exercise some degree of judgment. The coincidence circuit, then quite popular in cosmic ray research, was one electronic element that had some decision-making ability. For a coincidence circuit to operate, several signals had to be fed into it at exactly the same time. If all signals didn't arrive together, the circuit didn't work. It was, in effect, rendering a judgment. When triggered by two or more inputs simultaneously, it said yes. But sensing only one signal at a time, it said no. A coincidence circuit in a cosmic ray telescope, for example, can be activated by detectors that serve the same basic function as the lenses in a conventional optical telescope. When all detectors are perfectly aligned with an incoming ray, they sense it at precisely the same instant, causing the coincidence circuit to fire. On the other hand, if the detectors are not aligned, the ray strikes some detectors before others and the circuit doesn't operate.

Mauchly wondered if the principles that governed the operation of coincidence circuits could be applied in the design of logic modules for an electronic computing machine. He also speculated about reworking some of the circuits in other kinds of instruments so that they would be able to add, subtract, multiply, and divide. If these elements were assembled in the right combinations, he theorized, the resulting system would compute. Mauchly kept on experimenting, and by early 1940 he had proved—at least to himself—that this could be done.

With the zeal of a missionary, he went forth to spread the good news. But his message went unheeded. Those who heard him thought that his plan for an electronic computer was a pipe dream that no one with any kind of scientific ability could take seriously. In fairness to his detractors, it should be noted that there was ample ground for skepticism. At that time, many electronic instruments were notoriously unreliable. The main problem was with the vacuum tubes, since the more tubes that were designed into a system, the more apt it was to break down frequently. Some instruments in cosmic ray research that used as many as 400 tubes would operate for only an average of twenty minutes before one would burn out and have to be replaced. Mauchly, however, wasn't proposing a few hundred tubes. His computer would need thousands. That many vulnerable parts would increase the probability of failure so much, said his critics, that the computer would never work. Turn it on and within a second or two a tube would blow out.

Certain that a way could be found to prevent this from happening, Mauchly kept on experimenting. Yet his efforts to get others interested met with no success until finally, one day in December 1940, he found a sympathetic ear.

John Vincent Atanasoff was a good listener because Mauchly's ideas were akin to his own. Atanasoff was in Washington attending a meeting of the American Association for the Advancement of Science when Mauchly, who was a speaker on the program, alluded to some of his ideas on computing. Atanasoff listened with great interest, and at the conclusion of the session, he went up to Mauchly and introduced himself. It seemed that Atanasoff, who was then a professor of physics and mathematics at the University of Iowa, was something of a computer buff himself.

In the early 1930s Iowa was one of the few universities in the country with an established reputation in computation. It had become an important center for mathematical statistics as the result of early work there by Henry Wallace, who later became secretary of agriculture and vice president of the United States during Franklin D. Roosevelt's third term in office.

Experimenting with an IBM tabulator during the early 1920s, Wallace tried to show that mechanical computation equipment could simplify statistical work in agricultural studies and weather forecasting. Years later he described those days in a letter to IBM's Dr. Cuthbert C. Hurd: "In the late winter of 1923, I taught a course in machine calculation of correlation coefficients using a cheap key driven machine. In the concluding session of ten lessons I decided to demonstrate how the IBM machine could be adapted to correlation work. For this purpose, I used a truck from the farm to haul a tabulator from Des Moines to Ames. I never used an IBM machine as an aid to breeding work but I did use it for some time in trying to predict weather. While this was a flop, I think that . . . it had something to do with starting the [U.S.] Weather Bureau on long-range weather forecasting."

Atanasoff was one of several Iowa faculty members who, in the 1930s, carried forward the experimental work initiated by Wallace. Atanasoff, like Mauchly, believed that electronics was the wave of the future, a fact that prompted Mauchly to decide to visit Atanasoff in Iowa. In a letter to Mauchly in May 1941, Atanasoff wrote: "I think that it is an excellent idea for you to come west during the month of June. . . . As you may surmise, I am somewhat off the beaten track of computing gossip and so I am always interested in any details you can give me."

While getting ready for his trip to Iowa, Mauchly heard about a program that might improve his chances for a job in industry. It was a six-week cram course sponsored by the University of Pennsylvania. Organized mainly as a mathematics and physics refresher for those who had earned degrees years earlier, it was also designed to sharpen electronic engineering skills, which were then in brisk demand in defense work. For Mauchly it seemed made to order. He mailed an application and then set out for Iowa. When he got there, Atanasoff and a graduate student were assembling some computing apparatus. Mauchly never saw it operate because three days later, a telegram from home brought good news. His application for the summer course had been accepted. Hastily bidding good-bye to Atanasoff, Mauchly headed back to Pennsylvania.

CHAPTER 3

An Idea in Limbo

By 1941 the small Philadelphia college founded two centuries earlier by Benjamin Franklin had become a huge academic complex. Abutting the twisting Schuylkill River and extending well into the western section of the city, the University of Pennsylvania had gained much renown through the years for its progressive programs in science and engineering. Growth, particularly after 1900, came largely from the administration's prudent management of resources and from a steady flow of gifts and bequests. One pivotal bequest during this period was from the estate of Albert Fitler Moore, a wealthy Philadelphia businessman.

The company that Moore headed was formed in 1820 when Moore's grandfather began manufacturing stays for ladies' bonnets and hoop skirts. In 1844 some measure of fame came to the family when wire made by the Moores was strung from Baltimore to Washington, enabling Samuel F. B. Morse to tap out his legendary telegraph message: "What hath God wrought?"

When Moore died in 1922, he left the bulk of his estate

to endow a memorial to his parents, specifically, a school of electrical engineering. The trustees of his estate, believing that any new engineering school would be dangerously vulnerable on its own, persuaded the court to award Moore's legacy to the University of Pennsylvania. And so, in September 1923, the "Moore School" was established, replacing an electrical engineering program that had achieved department status just ten years earlier. Harold Pender, chairman of the Department of Electrical Engineering, became the new dean. Pender, a brilliant scientist, had already gained international recognition for being the first to demonstrate

The Moore School of Electrical Engineering, University of Pennsylvania, Philadelphia, in September 1941.

quantitatively that a moving electric charge produces a magnetic field.

Classes met initially in the university's engineering building where a new west door, capped by an inscribed stone tablet, was built. Under Pender's leadership, the Moore School flourished, and in 1926 it was moved into a spartan brick structure on the edge of the campus at Thirty-third and Walnut Streets. The building had previously been occupied by a musical instrument company, a fact that prompted many students to refer to it as the "whistle factory."

One of those students was J. Presper Eckert, Jr., a member of the class of 1941. At age twenty-two, Eckert had clearly established himself as a comer. Intellectually aggressive and imbued with a drive to excel, he was not content to sit on the sidelines and watch others score points. As a young child, even before starting school, he displayed a budding interest in technology that led him to sketch pictures of radios and electrical gadgets while others his age were playing cowboys and Indians. And by the time he was a teenager in the prestigious Penn Charter Academy, he had designed and built a powerful sound system for the school auditorium that incorporated many features that wouldn't be available in commercial amplifiers for years to come.

While Eckert was growing up there, Philadelphia was the hub of America's electronics industry. Philco, a major manufacturer of radio receivers, had a large factory in the city, and just across the Delaware River in Camden, New Jersey, the Radio Corporation of America was amassing the resources from which RCA would later propel itself to prominence as a kingpin of the entertainment business. Less than a mile from the Eckert home was the laboratory of Philo T. Farnsworth, a gifted and prolific inventor whose patents would later be applied extensively in the development of television broadcasting. While still in high school, Eckert used to visit the Farnsworth laboratory and make himself useful by copying notes and performing other mundane tasks. For these services, he was sometimes paid in cash, but most of the time he opted for his pick of the many discarded parts no longer needed in the experiments. These prized possessions were carried home where they were put to use in his basement workshop.

From the beginning there was never any question in Eckert's mind about his future—he would become an engineer. In 1937 he entered the Moore School, and after graduating near the top of his class in 1941, he was awarded a two-year fellowship with an annual stipend of $400. His first assignment was to oversee the laboratory sessions of a new summer program. Although it had been customary for new instructors to get their feet wet teaching young freshmen, mostly in their teens, the class drawn by Eckert was different. The students were older and many held advanced degrees. Eckert's job was to provide guidance and help, when needed, in setting up the apparatus. However, one member of the class never asked for any assistance. John Mauchly didn't need to since he had done many of the same experiments over and over again during his eight years as professor of physics at Ursinus College.

Eckert could see that lab work was a waste of time for Mauchly. So when the other students didn't need him, he and Mauchly would sit and talk. At first, it was idle chit-chat, but that soon changed when Mauchly brought up his computer ideas. Much to Mauchly's delight, Eckert was surprisingly open minded about them. In fact, Eckert said he could see no technical barriers preventing the design of circuits that would do the things Mauchly was talking about. At this point, their conversations began to extend beyond the scheduled lab sessions; and they would adjourn to a nearby cafeteria, sketching ideas on paper napkins, while Mauchly sipped coffee and Eckert indulged his weakness for ice cream sodas.

Thoroughly enjoying his talks with young Eckert and basking in the intellectual ferment in the Moore School,

Mauchly forgot his intention to look for a job in the defense industries. Instead, on August 6, 1941, he wrote to Dean Pender: "I ask that I be considered for appointment to the teaching staff of the Moore School. For the last eight years, I have been the head of the Department of Physics at Ursinus College. My rank has always been Associate Professor. . . . Although I look forward to promotion to full professorship in the next few years, it seems to me that my opportunities for ultimate advancement will be better elsewhere." Following this preamble, Mauchly described his work at Johns Hopkins and his connections in Washington scientific circles. The timing couldn't have been better. Two professors had just left for military service and they had to be replaced. Although the draft was expected to cut into future civilian enrollments, special training programs for military personnel would keep classrooms filled.

A month later, Mauchly moved into an office at the Moore School recently vacated by Prof. Irven Travis, a Navy reservist called to active duty. Along with his books, Mauchly brought notes and files compiled during his experiments and a small switching circuit he had designed. He put the circuit on a table behind his desk. During the year that followed, its flickering tube would be a lonely beacon, the only tangible evidence of a new age in the making.

Mauchly's crusade for an electronic computing machine had won Eckert's allegiance, but Eckert was a young, inexperienced assistant instructor and—in a structured faculty hierarchy—low man on the totem pole. Mauchly needed backers who had impressive credentials and who would stand up and say, "This makes sense. Let's do it!" To marshal support of that kind, Mauchly had to build a convincing case and one that would withstand the most penetrating scrutiny. In August 1942 he put his ideas on paper. His strategy was to win support for electronic computing as a viable engineering concept before he pressed for a commitment. Intentionally, the text was brief, only five typewritten pages, and was introduced by a low-key title: "The Use of High-Speed Vacuum Tube Devices for Calculating."

Mauchly began by comparing deficiencies of a known quantity, the mechanical differential analyzer, with the anticipated strong points of its electronic counterpart: " . . . the mechanical analyzer has an accuracy limited by the way in which slippage and backlash [of gears, wheels, and wire cables] enter into its operation, whereas the electronic device, operating solely on the principle of counting can, without great difficulty, be made as accurate as is required for any practical purpose." The ease with which various electronic components can be interconnected, he went on, makes it possible to set up new problems quickly. Of even greater significance, Mauchly pointed out, more electronic elements can be added easily to handle more complex requirements and "additional spare components can be kept in reserve and quickly interchanged with any component which fails to operate." In contrast, replacing parts in the mechanical analyzer was a cumbersome and time-consuming job.

In a mechanical calculator, one number is added to another by the movement of cams, gears, and ratchets. In Mauchly's proposed electronic version, a number represented by electrical pulses could be shifted about and worked on by moving the pulses through wire circuits. Numbers could be stored and processed in components called "registers." Mauchly explained: "When a number such as 1216 is to be [stored] . . . it is not necessary for 1216 counts [pulses] to be generated. Instead a total of ten counts would be sufficient: *one* in the thousands register; *two* in the hundreds register; *one* in the tens register; and *six* in the units register."

The largest number of pulses for any register would be ten—nine to represent the highest digit, which could be added to any register, and one more for the carrying operation (to the next highest register). In a computing machine equipped with ten registers, two numbers of ten digits each (3,687,892,489 and 2,157,389,113, for example) could be added in about the same time as two numbers of two digits each (say, 89 plus 74), because additions in all registers would be performed at the same time.

Multiplications would be "carried out by successive additions as in mechanical calculators.... [It makes no difference] how many digits one of the numbers has. The number has to be added a total number of times equal to the sum of the digits of the multiplier." Mauchly hinted at the speeds at which this might be done: "Existing electronic circuits are capable of counting electric pulses at rates in excess of 100,000 per second."

Mauchly then wrapped it all up with a practical illustration: "[In ballistics problems] when similar equations are numerically integrated using manually operated mechanical machines, no more than 100 steps are usually necessary.... This is because in the manual computation sufficiently exact results can be obtained from 100 steps only if the methods of proceeding from one step to the next are somewhat increased in refinement. On the other hand, simplicity of construction and operation in the electronic computer is achieved by utilizing only the simplest step-by-step methods, and then many more than 100 steps are needed to obtain the final accuracy. It is obvious, however, that by the use of even 10,000 steps at the speed of the electronic device, the time for the overall integration is extremely short [100 seconds], in comparison to the time required for an equivalent manual integration—at least several hours—and also quite short in comparison to the time required [15 to 30 minutes] to achieve a less accurate solution on a mechanical differential analyzer."

There it was—a challenging idea in a proposal that was received kindly and read with interest. Yet, for many months, the idea and proposal would languish in limbo.

CHAPTER 4

Click, Clack, Compute

Charles Babbage lived a century ahead of his time. Bursting with schemes for building computing machines, but thwarted throughout his life by the inability of artisans to make the precision parts that would bring those ideas to fruition, he died in 1871, an embittered old man. Although endowed with incredible energy and intellect, he was, nevertheless, considered a maverick by his peers in England's scientific circles and was not averse to single-handedly taking on the most respected institutions of his day.

His boyhood excursions into the world of mathematics were so successful that when he entered Cambridge at age eighteen, he knew more algebra than his tutor. While at Cambridge, he and some friends founded the Analytical Society, an organization with the avowedly lofty purpose of preparing its members to "leave the world better than they found it." According to his autobiography, Babbage first began thinking about mechanical computers in 1812: "One evening I was sitting in the rooms of the Analytical Society, my head leaning forward ... in a kind of dreamy mood with a table of logarithms lying open before me. Another member coming into the room, and seeing me half asleep called out, 'Well, Babbage what are you dreaming about?', to which I replied, 'I am thinking that all these tables might be calculated by machinery.'"

The first product of these musings came ten years later. In 1822 Babbage built his Difference Engine, a machine that computed polynomials to an accuracy of six decimal places. He then tried to build a larger Difference Engine with a capacity for twenty decimal places. His Majesty's Government underwrote part of the cost with a grant of 17,000 pounds, but the machine was never completed because no one could make parts that would conform to the specified tolerances. In 1833 Babbage outlined plans for an even more ambitious project—the Analytical Engine—a machine that, said Babbage, would operate at a speed of sixty additions per minute and be versatile enough to solve almost any type of arithmetic problem. But inasmuch as this, too, would require hundreds of precisely fitted cams and gears, nothing came of it.

Much of what is known about Babbage's ingenious designs must be credited to the writings of the gifted Ada Augusta, Countess of Lovelace and only daughter of Lord Byron. Lady Lovelace, born in 1815, was twenty-three years younger than Babbage. As a child, she was taken with a group of her mother's friends to see the Difference Engine. One of them, a Mrs. Augustus de Morgan, noted with penetrating insight: "While the rest of the party gazed at this beautiful instrument ... [with the same expressions] that some savages are said to have shown on first seeing a looking glass or a gun, Miss Byron, young as she was, understood its workings and saw the great beauty of the invention." The first description of the Analytical Engine to appear in print was in 1842, written by L. F. Menabrea, an Italian military engineer. Menabrea attended a lecture given by Babbage in Turin and later summarized the main points in an article, written in French. Soon after, Lady Lovelace translated Menabrea's text into English, amplifying and improving it with notations of her own.

Throughout his later years, Lady Lovelace was a great source of encouragement for Babbage, even aiding him in plots to raise money to finance the continued development of the Analytical Engine. These collaborations included, among other things, working together on elaborate mathematical systems for picking the winning horses at the local racetrack. Regrettably, none worked and both Babbage and Lady Lovelace lost considerable sums in the process.

A few years before he died, shaken by his failure to build a mechanical computer, Babbage wrote in his memoirs: "If, unwarned by my example, any man shall attempt so unpromising a task and shall succeed in constructing an engine embodying in itself the whole of the executive department of mathematical analysis, I have no fear of leaving my reputation in his charge, for he alone will fully be able to appreciate the nature of my efforts and the value of their results."

Babbage's Difference Engine remained a museum curiosity until Howard Aiken, a rangy sharp-eyed mathematician, came along. One day in 1936, while leafing through some old scientific papers, Aiken was struck by the similarities between his thinking and the designs proposed by Babbage. A power engineer for twelve years before he decided to go back to school in 1935, Aiken enrolled first at the University of Chicago and then at Harvard as a graduate student in physics. It was during this period that thoughts about building a high-speed automatic calculator began to take shape in his mind. His doctoral thesis on the laws of space charge required him to laboriously hand calculate thousands of nonlinear equations. Plodding through them, he became obsessed by the notion that there had to be a better way to do these onerous computations. By 1937 he was sure he had found it. In a twenty-two-page proposal, Aiken outlined his idea: build a computing machine comprised of electromagnetic components and automatically controlled by a coded sequence of instructions that would rapidly spew out solutions punched in cards or printed by typewriters hooked to the machine.

Aiken, by then a faculty member at Harvard, seemed to be in the wrong place to promote such a thing. At that time Harvard was a center for "pure" research, and many believed that this was not the kind of project in which a university should get involved. What's more, said his colleagues, in a system so large and complex some part of it would always be breaking down; its components would be failing faster than they could be replaced. But Aiken was not easily dissuaded. Plucky and persistent, he had, throughout his life, surmounted obstacles that would have overwhelmed others.

Many years earlier, for example, his family's limited resources made it necessary for him to go to work after finishing the eighth grade. He got a job as a switchboard operator in the Indianapolis Light and Heat Company, where he was on duty twelve hours a night, seven days a week. During the day he attended Arsenal Technical High School. Somehow, his round-the-clock work and study schedule came to the attention of the superintendent of schools, who, when Aiken was in his senior year, arranged a series of examinations enabling him to graduate early. The same superintendent urged him to attend the University of Wisconsin in Madison and helped make that possible by using his influence to get a job for Aiken with the gas company there. In 1923 Aiken graduated and was immediately promoted to chief engineer of the company. He continued in power engineering work for many years before deciding, in 1935, to start a new career.

Unswayed by the opposition and skepticism that his computer ideas had stirred up at Harvard, Aiken looked for backers elsewhere. One of his first contacts was the Monroe Calculating Machine Company. He went to its chief engineer, G. C. Chase, and presented his case. Chase was impressed. Believing that Aiken's proposal could create new business opportunities for Monroe in the future, Chase went to his management and tried to persuade them to back it. But they turned it down, saying it was too impractical. Chase then suggested that Aiken go to International Business Machines, using Prof. Ted Brown of the Harvard Business School as an intermediary. Brown and astronomer Harlow Shapley were members of a very small minority at Harvard who saw some merit in Aiken's proposal. Brown subsequently arranged a meeting with IBM president Thomas Watson, Sr., which eventually led to the signing of a contract in 1939 that stated IBM would build the machine under Aiken's supervision and with the financial support of the United States Navy. The navy became a party to the agreement because the Mark I, as Aiken's computing machine would be called, offered great potential for expediting the growing volume of mathematical calculations in navy projects.

Work began in IBM's Endicott, New York, laboratory under a team headed jointly by Aiken and IBM's Clair D. Lake. (Other key members of the team were D. M. Durfee, F. E. Hamilton, and J. W. Bryce.) The machine they built was basically electromechanical—mechanical parts, electrically controlled. Although Babbage had relied on the intricate meshing of gears, Aiken used ordinary telephone relays, small devices in which thin metal strips affixed to springs can be moved a fraction of an inch by the pulling power of an electromagnet. When the current activating the electromagnet is turned off, the strip (drawn by the spring) falls back to its original position, breaking or making contact with another strip that interrupts or completes a connection through which electricity can flow. Thousands of such relays and other components were assembled in a frame fifty-one feet long and eight feet high that was installed in a building at Harvard in February 1944. (After America's entry into World War II, Harvard and many other universities muted their "pure" research orientation in order to concentrate on military projects.)

Aiken, on leave from his post as associate professor of mathematics, was now Comdr. Howard Aiken, USNR, presiding full time over the operation. Several junior officers, with strong backgrounds in mathematics, were assigned to help Aiken operate the Mark I. Richard Bloch, a young ensign, and Grace Hopper, a lieutenant in the WAVES, were among those developing the coding that guided the machine as it clacked through a problem. Bloch, who worked the night shift, sometimes rewired circuits and was not around to alert Grace Hopper when she came on duty the next morning. Unaware that a change had been made, she would put on a program and then the machine, its relays clicking like a thousand knitting needles, would suddenly stop. If Aiken was in the vicinity, he would rush over and demand, "Why aren't we making any numbers?" Aiken also took a dim view of a routine developed by Bloch that exercised all the elements in Mark I—lights flashed, relays clacked, and printers churned out meaningless numbers. The routine put on such a great show that it was used frequently to impress visiting admirals and other dignitaries.

About the same time, several research projects for the army were being conducted in the same building that housed the Mark I. One day, Grace Hopper and a navy yeoman surreptitiously entered the army storeroom to liberate some graph paper. As they were looking about, Aiken loomed in the doorway and asked what was going on. When Lieutenant Hopper stammered an explanation, Aiken made no comment. Taking this as tacit approval, the yeoman lifted an entire carton of graph paper, the only one in the storeroom, and started to leave. Aiken stopped him and said, "I'll admit that maybe the army can't count, but they *can* tell the difference between some and none. You had better leave one pack."

While Aiken maintained that he learned more about computing from "old Babbage" than anyone else, it would be a mistake to conclude that Aiken built Babbage's machine. The mathematician and computer historian Henry Tropp explains why: "Without trying to detract from the fantastic accomplishments of Charles Babbage . . . he and Aiken differed in a very important way. Babbage evolved a series of technical concepts, first for building a difference engine and later for building the analytical engine, which he conceived in 1833. However, in every case, before any significant portion of his machine was physically completed, Babbage would go off into new and better conceptions. One has the image of wandering with this quirky British genius through an infinite series of rooms, each representing some new and yet unfinished level of machine development. With Aiken, however, his Mark I was conceived in the mid-1930s, articulated very carefully and precisely, and built almost to specifications with, moreover, materials already on hand."

The computing potential of ordinary telephone relays was also foreseen, appropriately enough, by the telephone company itself. One Friday afternoon in 1937, George Stibitz, a mathematician in the Bell Telephone Laboratories in New York City, retrieved some discarded relays from a scrap bin there and brought them home for a weekend project. He wanted to test an idea. The fact that only ones and zeroes are used in the binary numbering system (compared to zero through nine in the decimal system) seemed to make binary notation ideal, thought Stibitz, for the two-state qualities of the relay.

With materials spread out on his kitchen table, he went to work. He attached two relays to a breadboard, wired a circuit around them, and improvised a way to get information into the circuit by opening and closing metal strips, cut from a tobacco can. A dry-cell battery powered the electromagnets in the relays, and two flashlight bulbs, each of which denoted a binary one when lit and a binary zero when dark. His intention was to make the relays give the sum, in binary, of two one-digit numbers. Much to his delight, he succeeded, and on the following Monday he took his toy into the labs in order "to show it to some of the boys [who] . . . were all more amused than impressed." Their amusement failed to dampen his enthusiasm, and he continued, during spare time at home, to sketch more circuits, which he believed could add, multiply, and even divide in binary.

Months later, Dr. T. C. Frye, Stibitz's superior at Bell Labs, who had been brought into a project involving many complex numbers, asked Stibitz if the calculating circuits Stibitz had been working on would do complex arithmetic. They certainly could, replied Stibitz: "I had already thought out most of the components for a complex calculator, and so soon I had drawings sufficiently complete to be considered. . . . Since I knew nothing of the well developed switching [telephone] art, my sketches must have amused the switching engineers. But—there was Sam Williams."

Williams, a switching engineer with many years' experience, was asked to look at the Stibitz sketches. While quite at home in the realm of relays, Williams was in strange territory when it came to the Stibitz brand of mathematics and number theory. In the beginning it was a struggle for him to decipher the drawings and cope with the intricacies of binary notation. But he soon got the hang of it, and in a few weeks, Williams made a thorough study of the proposal and reported that it was technically sound.

The matter was referred to higher echelons for review, and shortly thereafter, Stibitz got a green light to move ahead. The expertise acquired by Williams as he made his way through the Stibitz drawings also made him the obvious choice to prepare the final detailed design. In the fall of 1937, he and Stibitz set to work. One of their first decisions concerned input: How would data be fed into the machine? With calculations being carried out in binary, it would simplify things, they thought, if inputs were binary, too. But after a closer look, this idea was abandoned. While decimal input might create some sticky conversion problems, going that route appeared to be worth the trouble. Their reasoning was that later on, many young women would be trained as operators, and it would be far easier for them to use a familiar numbering system than to continually "think binary."

Stibitz and Williams worked throughout the winter, and by spring they knew—on paper, at least—precisely what their computer would do. It would have a capacity of eight

More than forty years after he built his legendary "kitchen table computer" on a weekend in 1937, George Stibitz reminisces about the unit (on the table) that successfully demonstrated his ideas for adding in binary with the aid of a simple logic circuit.

decimal digits with two extra digits in the arithmetic unit to compensate for excessive rounding-off errors when accumulating many subtotals. The average operating speed of the relays that were available at that time was around ten milliseconds. This meant that forty numbers could be added in about half a second. In order to make up for the sluggish response of a balky relay now and then, extra time was factored in. Although a calculation might theoretically require only half a second, circuits were designed to make the computer wait an additional second or two before going on.

The last relay was wired into place in the summer of 1939. Months of testing and debugging followed. To help pinpoint troublespots, Williams devised an ingenious diagnostic program that enabled the Complex Calculator, as it came to be called, to identify on a teletypewriter printout the exact locations of faulty relays and other subnormal parts. In January 1940 the job was finished. After three years of watching his dream take shape, it wasn't easy for Stibitz to let go: "When it [finally] was set up, Sam and I washed our hands and settled down to our customary work, pausing once in a while to go and peek at our baby, to make sure it was eating and sleeping well."

Stibitz was now itching to get started on a larger machine, but his suggestion that a follow-on calculator be built based on some new ideas he had was rejected. The initial venture into automatic computing had cost the telephone company $20,000—an astronomical sum in those days—and although no one could say that the effort was a failure, additional expenditures for another machine were out of the question.

But the money barrier crumbled when America declared war on the Axis powers in December 1941. Almost overnight, the Stibitz ideas were back in fashion. Stibitz was loaned to the National Defense Research Committee, the group formed by Vannevar Bush after his meeting with President Franklin D. Roosevelt. At NDRC, Stibitz

One of three operator stations at the Bell Laboratories facility in New York City for the "Complex Calculator" built by George Stibitz.

The keyboard of the first Bell Laboratories computer, completed in January 1940 by George Stibitz.

designed a dynamic tester for antiaircraft controls "which was actuated by a punched paper tape with digital information and which provided outputs simulating arbitrary motions of a target."

Next, with the blessing of NDRC, Stibitz designed a Relay Interpolator to produce the tape for the antiaircraft tester. The job of building it was turned over to Bell Laboratories. There, a team under the leadership of E. G. Andrews assembled a new computer, dubbed Model II. (The Complex Calculator had been designated Model I by this time.) Model II was completed and ready for business in September 1943. As Stibitz recalled: "It was exciting and a bit weird to watch it go about its work *sans* human boss, days, nights, Sundays, and holidays. . . . It could call for the next program step from one tape and the next data from another at exactly the right instant, and detect any extra holes worn in the tape by repeated runs. Those tapes took a pounding. . . . Sometimes we would come in on Monday morning expecting hundreds of feet of tape for the dynamic tester, only to find that one of the input tapes had worn through leaving the computer without instructions." Model II, nevertheless, was a resounding success. After providing much useful data for the dynamic tester, it was moved later in the war to the Naval Research Laboratories, where it continued to churn out tape until it was eventually retired from service in 1961.

Soon after Model II was up and running, four other models (III, IV, V, and VI) followed in rapid succession. Then, in 1950, for the second and final time, Bell Laboratories terminated work on the Stibitz computers. But the books couldn't be closed on thirteen years of effort without a bouquet for the first small binary adder that George Stibitz built at home on a weekend in 1937. Appropriately, it is identified in the annals of the company as Model K—the Kitchen Table Computer.

CHAPTER 5

The Moore School Connection

Standing in the basement of the Moore School, Lieut. Herman H. Goldstine patiently watched Joe Chapline replace a worn cable in the Differential Analyzer. It was March 1943 and Goldstine, as commanding officer of the Ballistic Research Laboratory's substation in Philadelphia, was faced with a backlog of staggering proportions. Every delay in compiling firing tables—even stopping the Differential Analyzer for routine maintenance—eroded his chances to catch up. Pacing back and forth in the narrow aisle, Goldstine muttered his concern about the state of affairs. He had to move things faster—but how?

Months earlier, word had gone out that more help was needed to keep the inner workings of the Differential Analyzer running smoothly. John Mauchly suggested a former student, Joe Chapline, whose penchant for dismantling and rebuilding old clocks seemed to make him ideally suited for the job. Chapline was hired, and now as he coiled the cable he was about to return the favor. Looking up, he told Gold-

The Differential Analyzer in the basement of the Moore School. Solutions to problems were recorded on charts mounted along the right side of the machine.

stine to see John Mauchly. Mauchly, he said, knows how to do this a thousand times faster—with electronics.

Skeptical, yet unwilling to leave any stone unturned, Goldstine hurried upstairs. He found Mauchly and quickly came to the point. Can you build an electronic computer? Yes. Well, why don't you write a proposal? I did . . . months ago. What happened? Nothing. Goldstine asked for a copy but none could be found. Then a secretary who had typed the original report ferreted an old shorthand book out of a drawer, located the notes dictated by Mauchly, and retranscribed them. Armed with this document, Goldstine went to Prof. John G. Brainerd, the Moore School's official representative in all matters involving the ordnance department. Goldstine asked Brainerd what he thought of Mauchly's ideas. Brainerd replied that "they were not unreasonable." Then, with Brainerd's blessing, Goldstine sped down to Aberdeen to see Maj. Paul Gillon.

Mauchly, elated by this unexpected turn of events, hoped for an early start on the proposal. Others were less optimistic. Goldstine, they said, was only a lieutenant with neither rank nor the influence to pull this thing off. But Goldstine had something more going for him. He knew that during wartime the army spent a lot of money on "long shots." Some panned out. Many didn't. No matter. If the potential payoff was big enough, it was worth the gamble. Goldstine was certain that the prospect of a hundredfold improvement in compiling firing tables was sufficiently enticing to capture attention at the right levels.

Goldstine briefed Maj. Paul Gillon, who, quickly seeing the merits of the Mauchly proposal, proceeded to smooth the way for a review by the top brass at Aberdeen. Soon after his conversation with Gillon, Goldstine was called on to make a presentation to a group that included Col. Leslie E. Simon, director of the Ballistic Research Laboratory, and Prof. Oswald Veblen, its chief scientist. While Goldstine theorized about the grandiose things that could be done with an electronic computer, Veblen listened intently, teetering on the back legs of his chair. Halfway through Goldstine's presentation, he tipped too far and both he and the chair crashed to the floor. Recovering, he arose and jabbing the air with his finger for emphasis exclaimed: "Simon . . . give Goldstine the money!" Then he turned abruptly and left the room. The meeting was over. The die was cast.

Days later, Brainerd, Eckert, and Mauchly hovered around a blackboard in a locked room at the Moore School. Mauchly's memorandum had been enough to start the ball rolling. But to maintain momentum, hard facts were needed: parts descriptions, costs, personnel, a construction timetable. Goldstine had asked Brainerd to produce a document covering these points by April 2, which was just a few days away. With chalk in hand, Eckert and Mauchly took turns at the blackboard blocking out answers to questions posed by Brainerd. This was the last of several sessions that had been conducted in secrecy earlier in the week. Finally, the draft was completed. Brainerd penciled in a few finishing touches and turned his notes over to a typist.

The report began by pointing out that: "There are mechanical differential analyzers at the Massachusetts Institute of Technology [6 integrators], at the Aberdeen Proving Ground [10 integrators], and at the University of Pennsylvania [14 integrators]. . . . In addition, the Massachusetts Institute of Technology is about to place in service a differential analyzer [18 integrators] having mechanical integrators but electrical connections. This analyzer is variously referred to as the Rockefeller Differential Analyzer, the electric differential analyzer, and the electronic differential analyzer. It should be carefully noted that the electronic differential analyzer discussed in this report has almost nothing, except purpose, in common with the 'electronic differential analyzer' at the Massachusetts Institute of Technology. . . . The electronic differential analyzer to which this report is devoted is one in which *all* operations are carried out by electronic circuits."

Having identified Mauchly's concept as an entirely new frontier in computing machine technology, Brainerd then made a dazzling assertion: A trajectory that takes up to two hours to plot on a mechanical differential analyzer could be computed in less than five minutes by its electronic counterpart. But what about accuracy? Brainerd had a straightforward answer for that question: "The accuracy [of an electronic computer] is limited only by the amount of equipment available." When more precision was needed, more circuits would be added. Adding equipment on a mechanical analyzer, on the other hand, had the opposite effect. With more cable slippages and meshing gears to contend with, answers became fuzzier when zeroing in on smaller and smaller increments. Errors would also be easier to detect, Brainerd maintained, because a mistake made by an electronic computer would be a big one. Therefore it "is much more likely to show because it will throw results far more out of line" than would other types of analyzers. Brainerd capped these rather stunning attributes by observing that an electronic computer "will not suffer in comparison with other analyzers with regard to time required to locate reasons for faulty operation ... [because the electronic computer] has the big advantage that faulty units can be replaced by spares in a very short time."

It was almost too good to be true. Yet beyond these arguments was a gaping void—there was no earlier experience to draw upon. A completely electronic computer—not even a small prototype—had never been built before. Mauchly's concept and Brainerd's proposal had to be accepted on faith. That was that.

The proposal was delivered to Aberdeen on April 2, 1943, and was immediately subjected to intense scrutiny by the staff there. Within days a list of questions was rushed back to Brainerd. A revised and expanded document was needed quickly—by April 9, in fact. High-ranking officers and some civilian advisers would meet at Aberdeen on that date to iron out final details preliminary to the awarding of a construction contract. Eckert and Mauchly went into seclusion and worked desperately to meet the deadline. They were up the entire night of April 8–9 and at dawn climbed into the back seat of Goldstine's car for the two-hour drive to Aberdeen. While Brainerd, in the front seat, chatted with Goldstine, Eckert and Mauchly continued to write, balancing note pads on their knees. When they got to Aberdeen, their jottings were turned over to a team of typists, Brainerd and Goldstine rushed off to their meeting, and Eckert and Mauchly were escorted to a small room where, for most of the day, they continued to churn out supporting arguments for the proposal. One of the main worries (which was discussed at length during the meeting attended by Brainerd and Goldstine) was the unprecedented number of vacuum tubes to be plugged into the new computer. The total, according to Mauchly, could go as high as 18,000. T. H. Johnson, who was Aberdeen's resident electronics expert, voiced much concern about the risks involved. Years later, Goldstine would acknowledge that Johnson had good reason to fret: "The proposed machine turned out to contain over 17,000 tubes of 16 different types, operating at a fundamental clock rate of 100,000 pulses per second. This means that the machine was a synchronous one, receiving its heart-beat from a clock which issued a signal every 10 microseconds. Thus, once every ten microseconds [ten one-millionths of a second] an error would occur if a single one of the 17,000 tubes operated incorrectly; [in other words] in a single second there were 1.7 billion chances of a failure occurring. . . . [The machine would have to] operate with a probability of malfunction of about one part in 10^{14} in order for it to run 12 hours without error. Man had never made an instrument capable of operating with this degree of fidelity or reliability."

Against such odds, success seemed light-years beyond reach. Johnson's logic, in any other time, would have knocked Mauchly's thesis into a cocked hat. But these, of course, were not ordinary times. While some likened the building of an electronic computer to grasping at a straw in the wind, the worsening situation in the production of firing tables convinced others that it was worth the gamble. In a secret memorandum to Dean Pender, Brainerd wrote: "In the specific case of sidewise firing from airplanes, construction of directors for guns has been held up several months because it has been a physical impossibility to supply to the manufacturers the necessary ballistic data. The proposed electronic difference analyzer would, if successfully developed, not only eliminate such delays but would permit far more extensive ballistic calculations than are now possible with available equipment."

Shortly after the meeting on April 9, Colonel Simon petitioned for the addition of $150,000 to the Ballistic Research Laboratory budget in order to fund the construction of an electronic computer. A few weeks later the request was approved, and on May 31, 1943, five days before a formal contract was signed, work began in the Moore School. Initially, the University of Pennsylvania would receive $61,700 to fund the construction of two accumulators (used to add and subtract numbers, up to ten digits each, and store the results) and a cycling unit—three major components that, when operated successfully, would trigger payment of the remaining balance for building the rest of the computer. This was a compromise of sorts. The "electronics" camp would now have a fair chance to prove its point. But should this first try fail, the project would be aborted, enabling the skeptics to enjoy the satisfaction of having helped cut the losses.

In a memorandum written on June 7 to his superior in the university hierarchy, Dean Pender reported that the name of the proposed machine had been changed to the Electronic Numerical Integrator and Computer (ENIAC). The memo continued: "Of the 21 persons whom we hope ultimately to have working on the project only three are members of our regular teaching staff; the others are members of our research engineering staff, project shop employees and others whom we hope to employ exclusively for work on the project. In the case of Dr. Burks and Dr. Witmer, we will transfer these men from other projects. They are carrying full teaching schedules. The same is true of Dr. Mauchly who, however, is listed as a full time research engineer because of my belief that his contribution will be the equivalent of such a person even though he carries a full teaching schedule."

Several research engineering staff members were immediately recruited for the ENIAC team. Eckert, having come a long way in a very short time, was undoubtedly the star of this group. Only two years after earning his degree in engineering, he had compiled an impressive record of achievements. In collaboration with P. W. Gumaer, for example, he designed and built an electronic sensor that used ultraviolet light to detect concentrations of naphthalene vapor. During the same period, he worked with John Clark Sime, Jr., on the development of equipment that determined fatigue limits in metals. Then, on his own, Eckert successfully conceived a device for measuring small magnetic fields, which was subsequently turned over to the navy and used in experimental studies of ways to detonate magnetic mines and detect enemy submarines. Next came a series of radar projects, including one that measured targets to an accuracy of one part in 50,000. And while all this was going on, he also designed new torque amplifiers for the Moore School's Differential Analyzer, greatly improving its accuracy.

This dazzling display of expertise, plus high marks for his work on the army proposal, catapulted Eckert into a key post on the ENIAC project. As chief engineer, he had the ultimate responsibility for converting Mauchly's ideas into reality. Meanwhile Mauchly, the senior consultant on the project, would be at Eckert's elbow every moment that he wasn't scheduled to teach a class.

Although the ENIAC project was not officially under way until June 5, 1943, Eckert and Mauchly had left the starting gate weeks earlier. Once assured that the army would endorse their proposal, both worked feverishly on plans to implement it. Eckert's first task was to devise ways to make the parts for ENIAC as failure-proof as possible. While suppliers of vacuum tubes and other electronic components usually sent along performance data, much of this information, in Eckert's view, was too primitive to rely on. Actually there was little incentive for anyone to do anything about this because frequent component failures, though bothersome, could be tolerated in mass-produced radios and electronic sound systems. Replacing tubes and parts was cheaper in the long run than hiking production costs with lengthy testing and quality-control measures.

Eckert's problems with the sketchy information from electronic parts makers were compounded by the fact that he could not find test equipment accurate enough to compile the additional data he needed. The only course open to him, he told Brainerd, was to stop everything and build the gear himself. Brainerd, feeling that Eckert's time and talent were too valuable to squander this way, recruited five technicians to do most of the basic work under Eckert's supervision. One of these was Herman Lukoff, an undergraduate student at the Moore School. Lukoff was trying to decide what to do during the six-week summer recess, his first vacation in more than two years. Some of his friends were being hired as field hands on farms over in New Jersey. Lukoff was intrigued when he heard this news. Working in fresh air and sunshine could be a very welcome change of pace. But he scuttled that idea when he was called into Brainerd's office and offered a job on a secret army project.

Lukoff was so excited that he accepted without asking what the pay was. A few days later, while his friends toiled in green fields elsewhere, Lukoff stood at a workbench in a Moore School laboratory listening to Eckert outline his assignment. His job was to build a signal generator that had a range of 20 Hz to 1 MHz and that produced four sine wave outputs, each continuously variable in phase from zero to 360 degrees. Eckert gave Lukoff some tips on how to do this and then stopped by once or twice a day to see how things were going. When Lukoff finished, his signal generator and some additional instruments built by other technicians were bolted onto a rack that had been mounted on wheels. Six of these rolling test units were completed before his vacation was over and he had to return to classes.

Lukoff, a senior, let it be known that he wanted to come back to the project after he graduated. In February 1944, after being awarded a bachelor's degree in electrical engineering, he was rehired. Work on the two accumulators was well under way, and Lukoff was told to design power supplies for them. The wide range of voltages needed for the various circuits in the accumulators required nearly twenty different power sources. Eckert, as before, monitored his progress, offering suggestions and guidance. Lukoff completed all the power units barely twenty-four hours before he was to report for induction into the navy. On that last day he held his breath and threw the switch. Everything worked. Glowing with satisfaction, he shook hands with Eckert, Mauchly, and Brainerd and set off for boot camp.

By June, after long and frustrating weeks of debugging, the two accumulators were finally operating reliably. Although Goldstine was in the hospital with infectious hepatitis, he managed to keep abreast of what was going on. In a letter written July 3, 1944, Dean Pender briefed him on the situation: "Operation of the two accumulator units has been a source of satisfaction to all of us. Some of the details have been described to you over the telephone. . . . The results of the tests have been gratifying not only in a general way but in very specific manners. For example, the actual operation has indicated that numerous types of subsidiary units which go into an accumulator have been properly designed. No major mistake has turned up. . . . The present situation is that we have two accumulators together with the necessary auxiliary equipment, so that we have been able to do such things as solve the second order differential equation for a sine wave and that for a simple exponential, as well as go through the processes of addition, subtraction, automatic repeated addition, etc. These we have been able to do at the rated speed of the machine, which is so rapid that it is impossible to follow the results on indicating lights. . . . On the whole I believe there is reason for moderate optimism . . . and I see nothing in the future which should be more difficult than has already been overcome in the past."

A few weeks later, Goldstine, now recovered and back on duty, stood alone at the railroad station in Aberdeen waiting for a train to Philadelphia. Only minutes before it was due, a man hurried by him, walked quickly to a spot about thirty feet away, and then peered down the track. It was John von Neumann, the world-renowned mathematician who was then a member of the Scientific Advisory Committee at the Ballistic Research Laboratory and, unknown to Goldstine, also a consultant to the top-secret atomic research center near Los Alamos, New Mexico.

Goldstine's first impulse was to rush over and introduce himself but he hesitated, fearing that von Neumann would think it an impudent intrusion. Finally overcoming his reticence, Goldstine drew closer and started talking. Goldstine recalls: "Fortunately for me von Neumann was a warm friendly person who did his best to make people feel relaxed in his presence. The conversation soon turned to my work. When it became clear to von Neumann that I was concerned with the development of an electronic computer capable of 333 multiplications per second, the whole atmosphere of our conversation changed from one of relaxed good humor to one more like the oral examination for the doctor's degree in mathematics."

Von Neumann, immediately grasping the significance of Goldstine's news, asked to witness a demonstration of the accumulators as soon as possible. One was quickly arranged, and while Eckert and Mauchly stood by, von Neumann watched the accumulators race through a problem he had brought with him. When presented with the answer, he exclaimed delightedly: "That's right!" From that day forward, the Moore School became a much visited way station in von Neumann's travels. Shuttling between Los

Alamos and Aberdeen or Washington, D.C. (where he was a consultant to the Navy Bureau of Ordnance), he frequently detoured up to Philadelphia for animated conversations with Eckert, Mauchly, and Goldstine.

By August 1944 Goldstine was confidently predicting that ENIAC would be completed the following January. Meanwhile, Eckert and Mauchly continued to generate new ideas that, if implemented, would be measurable improvements over their original designs. But changes take time and there was none to spare. The demand for firing tables was growing at an alarming rate. During one week in the summer of 1944, the computing branch of the Ballistic Research Laboratory completed ten gunfire tables, one bombing table, three aircraft fire tables, and one "miscellaneous major computation"—fifteen in all. But calls for new tables were coming in at a rate of more than forty a week. Under the weight of these pressures, Goldstine doggedly pushed ahead, trying desperately to get ENIAC on stream soon and lobbying for a second more advanced machine. In an August 11 memo to Colonel Simon, he urged that "a new contract be entered into with the Moore School to permit that institution to continue research and development with the object of building ultimately a new ENIAC of improved design."

Goldstine's proposal made sense because ENIAC's design was frozen. The wiring team had taken over, and there was little left for the engineers to get their teeth into. Goldstine's campaign for a second computer gained momentum in a letter written on September 2, 1944, to Colonel Gillon: "there are two further directions in which we should pursue our researches. . . . The switches and controls of ENIAC [which are] now arranged to be operated manually, can be positioned by mechanical relays and electromagnetic telephone switches which are instructed by a Teletype tape. . . . [With this arrangement] tapes could be cut for many given problems and reused when needed. . . . The second direction to be pursued is providing a more economical electronic device for storing data than the accumulator. Eckert has some excellent ideas on a cheap device for this purpose."

Indeed he had. A year earlier Eckert, collaborating with some Moore School associates, had experimented with another new device invented by William Shockley of Bell Laboratories. Eckert was now recommending a similar component as a memory for a second electronic computer. Shockley's delay line operated on the principle that ultrasonic signals move through fluids at much slower speeds than electric pulses through wires. The means for exploiting this differential was discovered by Pierre and Jacques Curie in 1880. The Curies found that a quartz crystal of the proper diameter and thickness vibrated mechanically when charged with electricity. They also showed that the converse was true: Make the crystal oscillate and electric pulses will be generated.

Eckert's plan was simple and ingenious. Mount quartz crystals at opposite ends of a one-and-one-half-meter tube and fill it with mercury, and then activate one crystal with fast-moving electric pulses (representing digits to be stored in the computer's memory). The vibrating crystal creates ultrasonic signals that move through the mercury at a much slower speed. When the ultrasonic waves reach the opposite end of the tube, they strike the second crystal, which oscillates and regenerates the original electric pulses. Every pulse coming out of the delay line is amplified and fed back to activate the first crystal, and the whole process is repeated. In this way, a continuously moving stream of 1,000 binary digits can be stored indefinitely. With appropriate vacuum-tube circuits, called gates, the stream of digits can be interrupted and read or new data inserted when needed.

The potential savings offered by this device were enormous. Storing one number in ENIAC (the equivalent of four binary digits in the delay line) required one vacuum tube. A thousand numbers, a thousand tubes. The delay line, however, needed only ten vacuum tubes for detecting and amplifying the output of the second crystal and generating new input pulses for the first. Now 1,000 binary digits (or 250 decimal numbers) could be stored in a delay line computer using only ten tubes, 240 fewer than required for the same memory capacity in ENIAC.

Brainerd, the chief administrative officer of the ENIAC project, seconded Goldstine's plea for a successor machine. In a letter to Colonel Gillon on September 13, 1944, he argued: "The progress of the work on ENIAC has led to some rather extensive discussions concerning the solution of problems of a type for which the ENIAC was not designed. . . . It is not feasible to increase the storage capacity of ENIAC . . . to the extent necessary for handling non-linear differential equations on a practical basis. The problem requires an entirely new approach. . . . A delay line could store a large number of characters in a relatively small space and would . . . enable a machine of moderate size to be constructed for the solution of partial differential equations which are now blocking progress in certain fields of research at the Ballistic Research Laboratories."

Gillon agreed. Five days later, his office authorized an initial expenditure of $105,600 to begin the design of a second electronic computer—a machine that eventually would be known as the Electronic Discrete Variable Automatic Computer, or EDVAC.

CHAPTER 6

Enter ENIAC

It was official. Japan had surrendered. The war was over, and military procurement officers scrambled to halt the flow of armament pouring from American factories. Telegrams canceling contracts went out by the thousands. Mountains of supplies, crammed in depots, were declared surplus and later sold for pennies on the dollar. Ships sailed homeward, headed for berths in the mothball fleet. Yet ENIAC, unfinished and months behind schedule, was spared. It was still needed.

Russia, technically an ally of the Western powers, was being watched warily by the free world. Because much of Eastern Europe lay under Russia's heel, the American military considered it prudent to maintain a posture of readiness, which meant that finding ways to speed up production of ballistic firing tables was still a matter of urgency for the army. And so, on September 7, 1945, John Brainerd, exhorting his project team to press forward, issued a new schedule to ensure that "work on the ENIAC itself will proceed from

8:30 in the morning to 12:30 the following morning except
... Sunday."

Progress had been agonizingly slow. Critical materials in
the quantities needed were hard to come by, and it took
some doing to parlay ENIAC's low priority (as a research
and development project) into authorizations for thousands
of vacuum tubes and other scarce parts. Once, after months
of waiting, a shipment of transformers and power supplies
arrived. They had been made by a well-known company,
noted for quality products. The entire lot when tested
proved defective, and substitutes had to be ordered elsewhere. Making the frames on which circuit elements would
be mounted required the services of a sheet-metal fabrica-
tor, and most were already swamped with war work. However, after a very long search, a small company that made
kitchen cabinets was located in New Jersey. It could get no
more steel and was going out of business. ENIAC's priority
was high enough to get some and keep the company operating a little longer.

While Eckert and his crew labored to breathe life into
ENIAC, a pair of physicists waited patiently on a desert out-
post nearly 2,000 miles away. In July 1945 Stanley Frankel
and Nicholas Metropolis, responding to urging by John
von Neumann, had interrupted their work at Los Alamos
to come to Philadelphia. Both were engaged in a top-secret
study of thermonuclear ignition, requiring thousands of
long and repetitive computations—the sort of thing, in von
Neumann's view, that the new machine could take on han-
dily. During their visit, and while technicians clambered
about, Frankel and Metropolis learned how to code and
write instructions. Back at Los Alamos a few weeks later,
they set out to organize their data in the required formats
and waited for word from Philadelphia.

The call came early in December 1945. Armed with
reams of data, Frankel and Metropolis returned to Philadelphia and, with the aid of several young women who had

been recruited to program and operate ENIAC, ran their problem. No one save Frankel, Metropolis, and Anthony Turkevich (another Los Alamos scientist who subsequently joined them) had any inkling of what it was because the numbers had been thoroughly camouflaged. In an affidavit for the U.S. Patent Office, dated January 31, 1962, Metropolis wrote: "The results which came off the machine were in the form of punched cards, containing tables of numbers only. There was no indication of what they were or what they were intended to represent. We had previously considered whether [anything] . . . could be inferred from these numbers and had decided that it would be extremely improbable for anyone to determine the nature of the problem or the results."

Neither Frankel nor Metropolis was expecting a solution and they didn't get one. The runs made on ENIAC were exploratory probings that they hoped would reveal whether additional research was justified. In due time they packed up and returned to Los Alamos, where they wrote a report recommending that "further and more complex calculations would be necessary and desirable."

Preparing ENIAC for a series of runs was an incredibly involved process. First, detailed instructions had to be written defining the problem and a procedure for solving it. These instructions were programmed by adjusting switches manually and inserting thousands of cables into as many as forty large plug boards. A team of five operators might work several days on the external wiring and many more days searching for errors and correcting them. Franz L. Alt, who was then a member of the technical staff at Aberdeen, recalls that once the final inspection was completed, "We would run the problem as long as possible. . . before changing over to another. Typically, changeovers occurred once every few weeks. . . . It was standard operating procedure to run every problem at least twice, for checking, and to run test cases at frequent intervals. Between runs there were

The ENIAC occupied a 30 × 50-foot room in the University of Pennsylvania's Moore School. Movable "function tables" in the foreground and right rear fed instructions to the computer while a problem was being solved.

Punched cards were the primary data entry and retrieval medium for ENIAC. Here, computer programmers operate the punched-card units that communicate with ENIAC through the huge cables connected to the processor banks (shown in background).

waiting periods for inspecting results, punching cards, and miscellaneous head scratching since it was impossible to switch problems on short notice."

Before ENIAC was later dismantled and moved to the Proving Ground in Aberdeen, Eckert and Mauchly devised a way to eliminate much of the switch setting and cable plugging prior to a new series of runs by putting instructions into the function tables. (Until then, the arrays of switches known as function tables were used only to store "six-figure values of two functions, with signs, or a twelve-figure value of a function . . . for each of 104 values of an argument.") The original idea for this procedure was documented by Eckert and Mauchly in a January 1944 disclosure of a magnetic calculating machine, later referenced in a September 1945 progress report on the EDVAC: "an important feature of [the proposed magnetic calculating machine] was that operating instructions . . . would be stored in exactly the same sort of memory device as that used for numbers."

EDVAC was a quantum leap forward in computer technology. Yet, in October 1945, a year after the ordnance command authorized development of a second electronic computer, EDVAC was just a "paper" machine. Most of the innovative ideas, coming after ENIAC's design was frozen, were still on the drawing boards. ENIAC, on the other hand, while lacking many of the new features planned for its successor, was nonetheless a stunning performer, churning through problems at the rate of 5,000 operations per second. Surely here was a feat worth shouting about from the rooftops, which was why the army and the Moore School began drafting an elaborate plan to publicize this achievement in newspapers and on radio on February 15, 1946.

But keeping the lid on until then proved difficult. On January 11, 1946, a story by Sidney Shallet in the *New York Times* revealed that "Plans have been presented to the

The function table (foreground) for the ENIAC is adjusted by a programmer prior to beginning a series of calculations for artillery firing tables.

Weather Bureau, the Navy, and the Army for the development of a new electronic calculator, reported to have astounding potentialities which, in time, might have a revolutionary effect in solving the mysteries of long range weather forecasting." Further on Shallet wrote: "Dr. John von Neumann who is associated with the Institute of Advanced Study and Dr. Vladimir K. Zworykin, associate director of RCA Laboratories at Princeton, outlined plans for the new machine."

This news hit the Moore School like a bombshell. Dean Pender hastily called a meeting after which Mauchly tried to reach Shallet to find out where and how he got his information. Goldstine was to contact Colonel Gillon in Washington to seek his help in plugging any future leaks. And nearly everyone wanted to talk to von Neumann, then in Princeton, but a telephone strike had virtually paralyzed communications along the eastern seaboard. Telegrams

Maj. Gen. G. L. Barnes watches Prof. John G. Brainerd program one of ENIAC's function tables.

were fired off to Washington, New York, and Princeton, but the Moore School was powerless to do anything more than wait and worry that this and other unauthorized disclosures would diminish the news value of the ENIAC demonstration a few weeks later.

The next morning (Saturday) a telegram from von Neumann was delivered that said he would be available to discuss the situation that afternoon. Eckert, Mauchly, and Goldstine drove immediately to Princeton and learned that von Neumann had no idea where Shallet got his information. Von Neumann, however, confirmed that he and Zworykin had given talks during the meeting in Washington the previous Wednesday. Von Neumann's only contact with the *Times* had been a call from a reporter (before the telephone strike) who, after saying an account of the meeting would appear in Friday's paper, asked if von Neumann wished to make a comment. Von Neumann replied that he

J. Presper Eckert, Jr., at the console of ENIAC prior to the public announcement in February 1946.

The public announcement of ENIAC, February 1946. Left to right: J. Presper Eckert, Jr., chief engineer; Prof. John G. Brainerd; Sam Feltman, chief engineer for ballistics; Capt. Herman H. Goldstine, liaison officer; Dr. John W. Mauchly, consulting engineer; Dean Harold Pender, Moore School of Electrical Engineering; Maj. Gen. G. L. Barnes, chief of Army Ordnance; Col. Paul N. Gillon, chief of the Research Branch of the Army Ordnance Research and Development Service.

did not, but before ringing off, the reporter intimated that a follow-up story on electronic computing might be published in the Sunday issue. Alarmed by the possibility of another leak in print before the ENIAC announcement, Mauchly caught the next train to New York to see if anything could be done to kill it. At the offices of the *Times,* he scanned an advance copy of the Sunday edition and, much to his relief, could not find any references to electronic computing.

Unable to reach Shallet, but still determined to identify the source of his information, Eckert and Mauchly took a train to Washington early the following Monday morning. First they saw Colonel Gillon, seeking permission to visit the Army Air Forces Weather Service in the Pentagon to ask some questions. Gillon had no objection and they went off and found a Major Wexler, one of the participants in the Wednesday meeting. Wexler said he had suspected that the matters discussed then should not be released to the press and had cautioned those present about this. Neither Wexler nor others contacted by Eckert and Mauchly later that day were able to explain how Shallet knew about the meeting. After several calls to the *Times* bureau in Washington, Mauchly finally reached Shallet, who disclosed that the information presented by von Neumann and Zworykin had been released to him by a navy officer. Mauchly then persuaded Shallet to not write any more computer stories until he had witnessed the special ENIAC demonstration being planned for the press.

However, the *Times* gave that assignment to someone else. The front-page story on ENIAC in the February 15, 1946, edition appeared under the byline of T. R. Kennedy, Jr., a member of the *Times* staff based in New York. Kennedy began by describing ENIAC as "one of the war's top secrets, an amazing machine which applies electronic speeds for the first time to mathematical tasks hitherto too difficult and cumbersome for solution. . . . Leaders who saw the device in action heralded it as a tool with which to rebuild scientific affairs on new foundations."

Kennedy's reference to new foundations was prophetic because the public demonstration of ENIAC proved to be a watershed for two diverging schools of thought on the future use of computers. One camp, led by von Neumann, viewed them as mathematical research tools for academicians. Eckert and Mauchly, on the other hand, envisioned a host of commercial applications, some of which were cited by the *Times:* "In the field of peacetime activities, Dr. Mauchly foresees [computers helping to design] better airplanes, gas turbines, microwave radio tubes, television, prime movers and projectiles operating at supersonic speeds carrying cargoes in space."

Von Neumann, who saw a way to revitalize the study of mathematical theory by introducing an exciting new dimension, had been quietly campaigning for a computer project of his own since early 1945. While he was then an adviser on several scientific and government committees, his employer was the prestigious Institute for Advanced Study in Princeton, New Jersey. The intellectual environment there barred involvement with the practical or the commercial, and distinguished scholars were invited to join its faculty not to teach but to think, an occupation that prompted the celebrated physicist J. Robert Oppenheimer to call the institute an "intellectual hotel."

For von Neumann to continue enjoying the stimulating companionship of his colleagues at the institute while dabbling on the side with an electronic computer would be like having his cake and eating it, too. The fact that the director and trustees of the institute would seriously consider such an arrangement is evidence of the stature von Neumann had achieved there and throughout the American academic community. Von Neumann's predilection for occasionally interrupting sojourns in mathematical theory for some practical work in a laboratory was a personal characteristic that some major universities played upon to lure him away.

In a letter written March 24, 1945, von Neumann's good friend Norbert Wiener tried to recruit him for a post at the Massachusetts Institute of Technology: "[Oswald] Veblen told me about your post-war plans for hydrodynamics. I think your balance of pure and applied mathematics is the right one [but] how does all of this fit in with the Princetitute? You are going to run into a situation where you will need a lab at your fingertips and labs don't grow in ivory towers. Mind you, I could stand a little ivory tower myself, and don't see you in any hurry to get out of one. If however you see yourself in the position of effective loss of your own non-ivory-tower schemes for the future, I have a secret to convey. A few weeks ago, Harrison, dean of science at M.I.T., asked me what the math department at M.I.T. would think about the possibility of you as head of the department.... I said, of course that would be delightful but didn't see what we could offer to compare with what you've got. The other day H. sounded me out again, to see if I had felt you out. ... We all want you and I am sure that someone can be found to relieve you of a large share of the routine administrative responsibilities, leaving you the policies and your favorite projects. ... It would be a great privilege to work close to you. You would automatically put us on top of the heap, and force Harvard into some strange antics of face-saving."

Harvard, of course, would not sit idly by and be left out in the cold. When he learned that the overseers had authorized the filling of some key vacancies on the Harvard faculty in early 1945, Prof. Marshall H. Stone proposed by letter from India that a "persuasive invitation" be tendered to von Neumann. Other members of Harvard's mathematics department made similar independent recommendations. About the same time, von Neumann was also being courted by the University of Chicago. Chancellor Robert M. Hutchins offered von Neumann a tempting package: a professorship as well as an opportunity to organize an "Institute of Applied Mathematics to be connected with the new Research Institutes of the University and which, among other things, would develop and construct a new high-speed automatic computer."

From the outset von Neumann viewed these propositions as second choices. During the spring and summer of 1945, he used all the persuasive powers at his command to sell his computer proposal to the institute's director, Dr. Frank Aydelotte. In doing this, he did not conceal the overtures by others but adroitly used them to convince Aydelotte that if von Neumann did not get his way, he would go elsewhere.

Attempting to buy time and postpone von Neumann's decision, Aydelotte wrote to those vying for his services at MIT, Harvard, and the University of Chicago. A letter sent to von Neumann on August 23, 1945, by MIT's dean of science, George R. Harrison, reports on this tactic: "I had a very kind letter from Dr. Aydelotte and quite appreciate his desire to look thoroughly into the situation at the Institute for Advanced Study and to keep you there if possible." Harrison then expressed concern that Aydelotte's effort to raise funds for the computer project might enable the institute to make an offer that von Neumann, in good conscience, could not refuse: "There is one possibility which bothers me a little. I would not like to see you get into the position of waiting a few months to see whether the Institute for Advanced Study decides to go in for high-speed computing devices or not, have them decide to do so and raise money for such a project, and then feel that since they had carried out their side of the bargain, you must automatically decide to stay." Harrison quickly moved on to the hard sell, pointing out that MIT was far better equipped than the institute to support a computer development program: "Certainly

Maj. Gen. G. L. Barnes reviews ENIAC maintenance record book with John W. Mauchly (left) and J. Presper Eckert, Jr.

the project involves a great deal more than merely raising the necessary funds. Here at MIT, as you know, we have a considerable background of experience in projects of this sort, and have already spent more than a million dollars in the construction of computing devices of one sort or another. As a result, you would find yourself immersed in a sort of 'potential field' which could only be built up over a long period of time in any institution starting fresh in the field of such projects."

Von Neumann did not neglect to tell Aydelotte that MIT was increasing the pressure. In his reply to Harrison, von Neumann said: "Many thanks for your letter of August 23rd which I have also shown to Dr. Aydelotte. I realize the validity of your arguments, and of course Dr. Aydelotte too is considering the problem from this point of view: Whether it is possible to finance and to organize in an adequate way and with adequate administrative and technical support such an enterprise here. . . . I realize the inherent suitability of M.I.T. for such projects, but at the same time it is clear that I should wait to see what the Institute for Advanced Study can create in this direction."

Nor did von Neumann hesitate to help Aydelotte in the search for funding. On October 16, 1945, von Neumann visited Commodore Lewis L. Strauss at the Navy Department in Washington, D.C., to solicit government support for building a high-speed computer at the institute. Two days later, during a conversation with von Neumann at Aydelotte's home in Princeton, Strauss asked for a more detailed proposal in writing. In a four-page response to this request, written October 20, 1945, von Neumann argued that while high-speed electronic machines "are now being built by various government agencies . . . and there is no doubt that the machines they aim to produce will be exceedingly useful in a wide variety of problems . . . it would [nevertheless] be an incomplete policy to develop such devices only for specific industrial or government laboratories, which have definite, and necessarily narrowly defined, applied problems to which they must devote all or most of the time of their equipment."

Von Neumann was lobbying for something quite different. He wanted to build "an electronic machine of the most advanced conceivable type" that, he emphatically declared, would not be used to solve applied mathematical, physical, or engineering problems. Rather, the computer itself would be the subject of experimentation and study in order to "develop new approximation and computing methods, and generally to acquire the mathematical and logical forms of thinking which are necessary for the really efficient operation of such a device. . . . I have no doubt whatever that we are on the threshold of very important developments both in pure mathematics and its applications, and that a pure research institution should spend several years in building a machine and experimenting with it. If we devote . . . several years to experimentation with such a machine, without a need for immediate applications, we shall be better off at the end of that period in every respect."

Von Neumann then reminded Strauss that the institute already had a contract with the Navy's Bureau of Ordnance for a theoretical study of high-speed computing machines. Von Neumann saw this as only a first step and that a well-integrated program was needed that would include the planning and building of a high-speed device for experimental purposes. He summed up his pitch with the assertion that one learns by doing: "A group which builds [a computer] is vastly better qualified to explore its possibilities experimentally than one which obtains it readymade."

A month later everything began to fall into place. A recommendation that the institute provide $100,000 in seed money for von Neumann's project was approved by the trustees. The Radio Corporation of America and Princeton University were brought in as cosponsors, and various other groups pledged support, including grants of $100,000 each from the army and navy ordnance departments. On November 20, 1945, von Neumann wrote a personal note to Norbert Wiener expressing regret that he would not be joining him at MIT: "The negotiations at Princeton have come to a conclusion [and] the Institute for Advanced Study, the Radio Corporation of America . . . and Princeton University have decided to undertake a joint high-speed automatic electronic computer development. While this is to be a community effort, it has been agreed the computer is to be located at the Institute and used exclusively as a research tool."

Recruiting a staff now became the first order of business. Von Neumann wanted to bring Eckert aboard immediately to help formulate the initial systems design and later to direct development work on the major components. But doing that required some finesse. Eckert was a prime mover on ENIAC and also a major contributor of design ideas for EDVAC. Both were funded by Army Ordnance, and von Neumann could not risk damaging his good standing with high government officials by pirating Eckert away from two of their projects. After discreetly advising Dean Pender of his intentions, von Neumann, in a letter written November 27, 1945, asked Eckert to join him: "If you decide to accept ... we will make ... the transition from your present work at the Moore School to your work with us smooth and gradual, extending over a few months, and we will endeavor to provide for mutual consultations between the staffs of the two projects on as broad a basis as possible, so as to interfere as little as possible with the Government's interests, and to secure the benefits of the exchange of ideas and of experience for both organizations."

Eckert, however, had other things in mind. Months earlier, he and Mauchly had visited officials at the Bureau of the Census in Washington, D.C., to tell them about ENIAC and to suggest that similar but more advanced equipment might be useful in their data-processing operations. That first visit was followed by additional meetings, and in the words of a report issued twelve years later by the bureau, the attitude at Census progressed from one of "casual curiosity to serious interest."

Eckert and Mauchly sensed that this growing support within the Census Bureau could lead to the signing of a contract and the establishment of their own computer business. They also had been approached by Thomas J. Watson, Sr., president of IBM, who offered them a chance to establish a new computing laboratory. Eckert was intrigued by this proposal because it promised freedom from the increasing institutional constraints that were limiting future options at the University of Pennsylvania.

The constraints were the inevitable results of new directions in policy. George McClelland, the university's president, believed that soliciting government support in the postwar period was inconsistent with his institution's academic goals and he did what he could to discourage it. Dean Pender, while not necessarily sharing this view because government contracts helped fund important work, became alarmed about laxities in the administration of the Moore School research programs and took steps to tighten things up.

By the time the news about ENIAC broke in mid-February, Eckert knew that his connection with the Moore School was nearing an end. Von Neumann's invitation to join the IAS team had not been answered but was still pending, visions of starting a computing laboratory at IBM grew more enticing day by day, and there was the possibility of going into business with Mauchly. Eckert favored accepting the IBM bid but Mauchly demurred, not wanting to become enmeshed in a corporate hierarchy. Mauchly saw a far more promising future for them as independent entrepreneurs, and he was supported in this stand by Eckert's family who, along with Mauchly, eventually convinced Eckert that this is what they should do.

Another action that influenced Eckert's decision to leave was Dean Pender's installation of Irven Travis as supervisor of research in January 1946. Travis, a former associate professor of electrical engineering at the Moore School, was a naval reservist who had been called to active duty in 1941. During the war he was a contracts administrator in the Naval Ordnance Department, and this experience, combined with his earlier key role in the construction of the Differential Analyzer at the Moore School, persuaded Pender that Travis was just the man to put things in order. One of his first moves was to promulgate a patents policy similar to those enforced by many industrial organizations. It required everyone to sign away his rights to any patentable ideas he developed while working on university research projects. Neither Eckert nor Mauchly would agree to this demand, and they resigned on March 31, 1946.

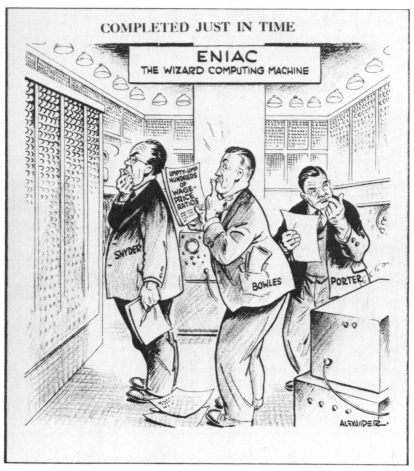

A newspaper cartoon *suggests that* ENIAC *might be able to solve the* perplexing wage-price problems *that faced Treasury Secretary John Snyder, OPA Administrator Chester Bowles, and Sidney Porter in February 1946 (from the* Philadelphia Evening Bulletin*).*

Several other members of the Moore School staff, resenting the new patents policy, let word seep out that they, too, were looking for greener pastures elsewhere. This disaffection came quickly to the notice of von Neumann as well as Eckert and Mauchly. Von Neumann, in fact, was drawn into a minor row with Travis over recruitment. When Travis learned that a member of the ENIAC project group had been in touch with Goldstine (who had joined the IAS team early in 1946), he wrote testily to von Neumann: "I received a memorandum from Mr. [Robert] Shaw stating that he wished to be released . . . and that he understood that you would write to me regarding the matter, and that further he expects to work for the Institute for Advanced Study. It seems therefore that I have no choice but to accept his resignation. . . . I must add however, that with the transfer of Dr. [Arthur] Burks, Mr. [John] Davis and Mr. Shaw from the Moore School to the Institute for Advanced Study, the cooperative effort required by the contracts which the respective institutions have accepted becomes increasingly difficult of attainment. . . . I ask that in the future you discuss with me first, rather than the individual concerned, matters of his possible transfer from the Moore School to the Institute and in particular that we agree upon salary scales and other inducements which, if they are not reviewed, may force us into unfortunate competition rather than the close cooperation . . . which is demanded by General [Gladeon L.] Barnes."

Von Neumann, bristling at the inference that he was off base in the Shaw matter, hastily replied: "It is our understanding that Mr. Shaw informed you at the time Messrs. Eckert and Mauchly left that he did not intend to remain in the employ of the Moore School but that he intended to go to work with those gentlemen. Late in the evening of May 4th, Mr. Shaw telephoned Dr. Goldstine to tell him that he did not intend working for Messrs. Eckert and Mauchly and inquired as to the possibilities of employment at the Institute. . . . We did not solicit [Mr. Shaw] to change his place of employment and, in fact, I do not believe I have even met Mr. Shaw. He has, however, expressed to Dr. Goldstine his wish to resign from the Moore School and to seek employment elsewhere. Under these conditions, it would seem quixotic of us not to attempt to secure so valuable a man. I am, accordingly, writing to Mr. Shaw offering him a position with our computer project."

At the time Shaw called, von Neumann's venture was in excellent shape. He had won approval to build his computer at the institute. RCA, with its vast technical and financial resources, had pledged valuable support. And the United States Government was about to begin awarding a series of research and development contracts. Eckert and Mauchly, on the other hand, had none of this. Their many pilgrimages to Wall Street won no converts. Not even the most daring venture capitalists wanted to take a flyer on a machine loaded with vacuum tubes and costing hundreds of thousands of dollars. Their one plus in a sea of minuses was the Census Bureau. But the officials there, while warming to the ideas they proposed, offered nothing more tangible than moral support. But there were other nibbles.

One was by Bryan Field, the manager of Delaware Park, a racetrack in the Diamond State. Field was looking for a way to dislodge American Totalisator Company from its grip on the American pari-mutuel betting machine business. Its virtual monopoly enabled American Totalisator to rent equipment to racetracks for a handsome fee—sometimes as much as one-half percent of the gross passing through the pari-mutuel pool. At Delaware Park, one of the smaller tracks in the circuit, the gross for a single day was usually about a million dollars. Consequently, during the course of a month's racing, the system installed there (attended by one full-time technician) could generate as much as $150,-000 in revenues for American Totalisator.

In 1961 former ENIAC programmers Betty Holborton (left) and Kathleen McNulty (then Mrs. John W. Mauchly) check an accumulator panel that had been rewired for an exhibit at the U.S. Military Academy, West Point, New York.

When Field read the news about ENIAC in the *New York Times,* he dashed off a letter to Eckert and Mauchly, inviting them to come down and see if a computer could be built to replace the American Totalisator machine. Because Delaware Park was not open then, Eckert and Mauchly visited the track at Havre de Grace, Maryland, as Field's guests. They saw very little of the horses, spending most of the afternoon in an enclosure under the stands observing the pari-mutuel betting system. By the end of the day they concluded that, yes, an electronic computer could do the job. Field, elated, pressed for time and cost estimates, assuring them that the backers of Delaware Park, mostly men from wealthy families, could be persuaded to accept any reasonable proposition. However, there was a hitch: A special-purpose system would have to be designed for the pari-mutuel application. Because Eckert and Mauchly were unwilling to be sidetracked and delay achievement of their main objective, which was to build a general-pupose computer, Field's betting machine problem was left dangling.

Later, in the summer of 1946, at a planning meeting in Washington for a government seminar on computing machines, Howard Aiken asked Eckert and Mauchly how things were going. Mauchly replied that prospects for a Census Bureau computer contract were getting brighter. Aiken looked at them quizzically for a moment and said: "Boys, my tip to you is this. There's a lot of money to be found at the racetracks." Maybe there was.

CHAPTER 7

The Crypto Catalyst

Shortly before noon on a bright Sunday morning in June 1944, a German submarine cruised quietly beneath the surface of the Atlantic, 150 miles west of Cape Blanco, French West Africa. Its captain, who was eating lunch, had just noted in his log that he anticipated arrival in Brest, his home port, in a few days. Moments later, a salvo of depth charges bracketed the U-505, rupturing the outer hull. Convinced that the damage was too severe to attempt limping away, the captain ordered the sub to the surface where crewmen burst from hatches and jumped into the sea.

Meanwhile, in a brilliant replay of a well-rehearsed plan, a boat was lowered from the U.S.S. *Pillsbury* and sped toward the U-505. Within minutes a boarding party led by Lt. (jg.) Albert L. David clambered aboard the abandoned sub. David, accompanied by petty officers Arthur K. Knipsel and Stanley E. Wdowiak, slid through the conning tower hatch and down the ladder and dashed forward to the radio room. There the three tore doors from lockers, seized cryptographic equipment, code books, and documents, and raced back to the hatch where they passed their booty up to waiting hands in the conning tower. Because the Germans had not anticipated a boarding attempt nothing was jettisoned. The only routine precaution taken was the arming of demolition charges, which were set to explode when everyone was clear.

In less than fifteen minutes, the Americans had neutralized the demolition charges and brought the leaks under control. David was awarded the Congressional Medal of Honor for this exploit, and Knipsel and Wdowiak received the Navy Cross. The U-505 was towed back to the United States and after the war became a permanent exhibit at Chicago's Museum of Science and Industry. The code books and other cryptographic paraphernalia, however, were rushed to the navy's intelligence and communications headquarters at 3801 Nebraska Avenue, N.W., Washington, D.C.

The Nebraska Avenue site was a top-secret center for deciphering codes and coordinating Allied attacks on Axis submarines in the Atlantic. Every day, from early 1943 until the end of the war, scores of messages radioed from the German submarine command to U-boats at sea were also picked up by Allied listening posts in the Caribbean, Bermuda, and North America. Many of these messages were quickly decoded by navy cryptanalysts with the aid of complex electromechanical and electronic gear that filled several floors of two buildings on Nebraska Avenue.

These exotic systems were the handiwork of major American companies, such as Eastman Kodak, National Cash Register Company, and Bell Telephone Laboratories. It was a fortuitous arrangement. With allocations and priorities blocking access to commercial markets during the war years, private industry scrambled for lucrative navy contracts that kept factories humming and stockholders happy. And the navy, including the communications-intelligence wing at Nebraska Avenue, had the undivided attention of the finest scientific minds in the business.

The surrender of Japan, however, cast a different light on things. Although the navy was willing, even anxious, to continue awarding contracts for more sophisticated cryptanalytic equipment, many of its qualified suppliers politely declined. There were good reasons for this lack of interest. First, the market for nonmilitary goods, kept in check during the war, was now ripe for exploitation. Second, for some companies, doing business with the navy had become more trouble than it was worth. Classified projects required time-consuming security checks before new employees could be hired. Factories had to be protected to a far greater extent than would be needed for standard commercial products and, while the financial risk was minimal for a navy contractor, the potential profit was limited, too.

The defections from the ranks of Nebraska Avenue's high-technology suppliers strongly influenced the future careers of two young navy officers who were stationed there. Howard T. Engstrom and William C. Norris, preparing for their return to civilian life, had similar goals in mind. Both wanted, in one way or another, to continue working in the fascinating fields of electronics and cryptanalysis, and they considered two possibilities. The first was to remain in the Nebraska Avenue organization as civilian employees; the second was to start a business of their own, designing and building cryptographic equipment for the government.

Becoming entrepreneurs was the more attractive option. Consequently, with the encouragement of brother officers, they went to see Capt. Joseph N. Wenger, who headed the navy's cryptanalytic operations in Washington. Wenger listened sympathetically to their plan, seeing the advantages in supporting a civilian engineering group with expertise gained during service as navy cryptanalysts. Although Wenger was receptive, he made no promises. Before he or anyone else in authority could deal with Engstrom and Norris, both would have to show that they had the resources and the staying power to become viable navy contractors.

Late in 1945 Engstrom and Norris were joined by another reserve officer, Capt. Ralph L. Meader, who had been won over by their plan to do business with the government. Meader had headed the Naval Computing Machine Laboratory, a special research and development unit that occupied facilities provided by the National Cash Register Company in Dayton, Ohio. NCR, a valued cryptographic equipment maker during the war, was one of the companies that the navy wanted to retain as a supplier. But NCR got out of the code machine business, choosing to concentrate its resources in the production of cash registers.

With the competition picking up its marbles and leaving the game, the going should have been easier for Engstrom, Norris, and Meader. But it wasn't. While Eckert and Mauchly were being laughed out of banking offices because their proposal to market huge electronic computers seemed too farfetched to be taken seriously, Engstrom and his colleagues were being shown to the door because they said too little. This was no time to be tight-lipped, but much of what they knew about cryptanalytic devices was classified and could not be divulged. Potential lenders could be told only that the three former navy officers planned to form a company to design and build advanced technology systems for the government. What kind of systems, the bankers asked. We can't tell you, was their reply. Meeting adjourned.

With Engstrom and Norris running into blank walls, some of their Nebraska Avenue associates, whom they had persuaded to wait on the sidelines until financing could be arranged, were becoming restless. In fact, the skilled reserve cadre of engineers and cryptanalysts was on the verge of breaking up when John E. Parker, a successful businessman and investment banker, was introduced to Meader by a mutual friend.

Four years earlier, Parker had founded a company in St. Paul, Minnesota, that became the second largest producer of wooden gliders for the army during World War II. By September 1945, however, his Northwest Aeronautical Company, having delivered more than 1,500 military personnel carriers for Allied airborne assault operations, no longer had a buyer for its one and only product.

When he met Meader, Parker was on the lookout for a hot new business idea. Meader's veiled references to an advanced technology enterprise aroused Parker's curiosity, and he promptly sought out Engstrom and Norris who, being subject to the same constraints that bound Meader, could add little more. Parker wanted in but he was no fool. Before commiting any resources, he had to be shown that there was a bona fide market for the mystery products being alluded to. A meeting was eventually arranged at the Navy Department, where senior officers from Nebraska Avenue and the Naval Ordnance Laboratory assured Parker that if Engstrom, Norris, and Meader could secure adequate backing, the navy would give them all the business they could handle.

That did it. During the next few days, Parker met frequently with Engstrom, Norris, and Meader, and on January 8, 1946, a new company, Engineering Research Associates (ERA), was incorporated under the laws of the State of Minnesota. The technical founders—Engstrom, Norris, and Meader—received 50 percent of the stock. The other half went to an investment group headed by Parker, which put up $20,000 in cash and also provided a $200,000 line of credit. Parker became president of ERA; Engstrom, Norris, and Meader, vice presidents. With the ink barely dry on their contracts, Engstrom and Norris immediately began to recruit a technical staff, which was quickly installed in the nearly deserted glider factory on Minnehaha Avenue in St. Paul.

Although the navy was ready and willing to deal with their new company, government red tape tied them down at the starting line. ERA was new and untried, they were told. Therefore, it could not be a prime contractor on government projects. Parker sidestepped this obstacle by soliciting business in the name of his Northwest Aeronautical Company, which, though now only a corporate shell, enjoyed an excellent reputation in military procurement offices. ERA, after becoming a subcontractor of the glider company, eventually earned the credentials to become a prime contractor on its own. When that happened, the name Northwest Aeronautical faded into history.

Parker and his associates were now moving in a direction that would soon position them squarely in the type of business Eckert and Mauchly had been espousing—the production and sale of general-purpose electronic computers. With ERA's proven skills in electronics and the obvious need to broaden the new company's market base, this was sound business strategy.

Meanwhile, in England, cryptanalysis was also the catalyst that spawned a curiously similar line of computer development. It began in 1938 when Richard Lewinski, a young Polish engineer, contacted a British intelligence agent in Warsaw and offered to sell what he knew about Enigma, a cipher machine the Germans were using to encode messages. A few months earlier, while employed in a factory in eastern Germany, Lewinski had deduced that he and his fellow workers were fabricating parts for some sort of secret signaling device. A keen observer and gifted with an extraordinary mind, he surreptitiously memorized the configurations and assembly details of all the major elements in an Enigma machine. Then a routine security check uncovered the fact that Lewinski was a Jew, and he was fired and expelled from Germany.

When word of Lewinski's offer reached London, Col. Stewart Menzies, deputy chief of the British Intelligence Service, sought the aid of two experts who could be slipped into Poland to interview him. One was Dilwyn Knox, a crack cryptographer, the other, Alan Turing, the youngest mathematician to be appointed a Fellow of King's College in Cambridge. Turing, twenty-six years old at the time, had already achieved a prominence in his profession that few, twice his age, ever attained.

Turing's tour de force was a treatise on mathematical logic describing a theoretical machine that in later years came to be identified as the Universal Turing Computer. The fact that Alonzo Church, a prominent logician, was working in a related field at Princeton University influenced Turing to sail to the United States in the fall of 1936 to attend graduate school there. He was not disappointed. In a letter to his mother, he wrote: "The mathematics department here comes fully up to expectations. There is a great number of distinguished mathematicians.... von Neumann, Weyl, Courant, Hardy, Einstein, Lefschetz as well as hosts of smaller fry."

Turing's Ph.D. thesis, completed at the end of his second year at Princeton, got high marks from John von Neumann, who tried to recruit Turing as his assistant. But Turing wanted no part of such an arrangement. Instead, he sailed back to England and resumed his work at King's College. Shortly after his return, he was contacted by Colonel Menzies and briefed on the Lewinski matter. Within days after the meeting with Menzies, Turing and Dilwyn Knox were meeting with Lewinski in Warsaw. Menzies's expert emissaries were sufficiently impressed by the quality of Lewinski's information to recommend that the Polish engineer and his wife be smuggled out of Warsaw, which was then infested with scores of Gestapo agents.

Traveling with falsified diplomatic passports, the Lewinskis were taken via Gdynia and Stockholm to Paris, where the French secret service moved them into an apartment on the Left Bank. Working with a carpenter assigned to assist him, Lewinski assembled a remarkable wooden replica of an Enigma. Lewinski's mockup was an oversized version of the original design, which used two electric typewriters for input and output. The plain text of a message was fed into an Enigma by one typewriter and the cyphered text version was typed out by the other. The cipher code could be altered at will by merely inserting another key in the machine, a feature that made it possible to produce an almost infinite number of different cipher alphabets. Therefore, if one did not know which keys to use on prescribed hours, days, and weeks of the month, there was no way to unscramble the code.

Using Lewinski's mockup as a guide, Turing, Knox, and a few associates set to work at Bletchley Park, a huge estate about forty miles northwest of London, that had been taken over by the British Intelligence Service. The computer they built was a marvel of ingenuity. Nearly 2,000 vacuum tubes were crammed into its circuitry, and two synchronized photoelectric tape readers scanned data at a rate exceeding 2,000 characters per second. The Bletchley Park computer faithfully duplicated the performance of thousands of Enigma machines and also identified key changes by German cryptographers in the later years of the war. I. J. Good, Turing's statistical clerk at Bletchley Park in the early 1940s, summed up Turing's part in this effort many years later: "I won't say that what Turing did made us win the war but I daresay we might have lost it without him."

Breaking secret ciphers by running them through exotic electronic circuits, however, was not an idea entertained solely by the English and Americans. In 1940 two young engineers, Konrad Zuse and Helmut Schreyer, proposed such a scheme to the German authorities.

Five years earlier, while completing his doctoral thesis at the University of Berlin, Zuse was faced with many tedious hours of repetitive calculations, a task similar to the one that had started John Mauchly thinking about electronic computing. Zuse, who considered this part of his education a scandalous waste of time, became obsessed with the notion that such work should be relegated to machines, not men.

After completing his thesis and finding a job as a design engineer, Zuse continued to conjure up ways to substitute machine power for brain power, finally arriving at three basic conclusions that would radically alter the course of his life. The first was that by modifying the operating principles of a special-purpose calculator, one should be able to program it to perform any mathematical task. Second, to accomplish this, he proposed to abandon the decimal system used in most calculators and convert all numerical values to the binary mode. And third, he concluded that a general-purpose binary machine could be constructed much as a child's erector set is assembled with inexpensive off-the-shelf parts.

One day in 1936, Zuse informed his startled parents that he had resigned from his job in order to devote all his time to building a computer. This announcement called for more than a token measure of parental tolerance because Zuse, who lived with his mother and father, proposed to build it in the living room, the largest open space in their apartment. Starting on a table in one corner, he began to assemble parts and components until the machine, growing like Topsy, eventually occupied the entire room.

This huge contraption, which Zuse had named the Z1, was actually a rough test model for evaluating concepts that he wanted to try out before building a second, more ambitious version, the Z2. When Helmut Schreyer, a close friend who had followed the assembly of the Z1 with great interest, learned that Zuse planned to use electromagnetic relays in Z2 in place of the clumsy magnetic memory switches in Z1, Schreyer urged him to go one step further. Use electronic vacuum tubes, said Schreyer. Electromechanical relays, he argued, will only calculate a few digits per second, but tubes could be cycled hundreds, perhaps thousands, of times faster. Zuse seriously considered this approach for a while, but when he found that tubes would greatly increase the cost of the machine, as well as the possibility of more frequent failures, he finally opted for the relays.

Schreyer, however, who had been looking for a suitable topic for his doctoral thesis, built some experimental computing circuits and later started to write a paper on the feasibility of calculating with electronic components. When completed in 1938, it was read dutifully by his professors and then left to gather dust on a library shelf. With the outbreak of war in 1939, Zuse and Schreyer got another idea: They were convinced that an electronic computer would be an invaluable aid in speeding up the deciphering of codes. They called on several government offices and were interviewed by some lower-echelon personnel before being granted an appointment with an official who had sufficient authority to make a decision.

By this time it was mid-1940. France had been overrun and Adolf Hitler was anticipating an early capitulation by the Allies. After listening to their proposal, the official asked: "Can you build such a machine within six months?" Zuse and Schreyer looked at each other and replied that it would take a year, probably longer. The official threw up his hands and said: "That's too long. The war will be over by then." Zuse and Schreyer were hurriedly ushered out of his office.

CHAPTER 8

The New Entrepreneurs

John Mauchly was euphoric. A letter written by John H. Curtiss, assistant director of the National Bureau of Standards, arrived one morning in May 1946 with encouraging news.

Several weeks earlier, Census Bureau officials, lacking the expertise to evaluate the technical merits of Eckert and Mauchly's computer ideas, sought the advice and counsel of Dr. Edward U. Condon, director of the Standards Bureau. Curtiss, who had been recently appointed assistant director by Condon, was assigned to represent the Census Bureau in the negotiations with Eckert and Mauchly.

While the Curtiss letter was not an outright endorsement, Mauchly, reading between the lines, sensed that one would be coming soon. Curtiss wrote: "Members of the Bureau of the Census and the National Bureau of Standards have jointly considered the specifications which you and J. P. Eckert submitted for a general purpose electronic computing machine. . . . Both agencies are interested in having work begin on a machine of this type as soon as possible. . . . In the next few weeks one or more negotiated contracts will be let for projects leading to the design and construction of such a machine. Adequate funds, amounting to about $300,000, are being transferred to the Bureau of Standards for [this] purpose." Curtiss also added this sweetener: "Within a short time, a further sum of money, of comparable magnitude, will also be transferred to the Bureau of Standards. . . for development of general purpose electronic computing devices."

Unknown to Mauchly, however, bureaucratic roadblocks were being thrown up. The National Bureau of Standards could not, solely on its own authority, make a commitment of this magnitude without first listening to the recommendations of an outside expert. Curtiss's hands were tied until he called in a consultant. George Stibitz, whose earlier work at Bell Telephone Laboratories ranked him as an elder statesman of digital computing, was tapped for the assignment. From Mauchly's standpoint, the choice of Stibitz was unfortunate.

In November 1943 Colonel Gillon had conducted a confidential ENIAC briefing in Washington for the National Defense Research Committee. Afterward, Stibitz, who was a member of the NDRC, displayed some bias against electronic computing in a letter on November 6, 1943, to Warren Weaver, another member of NDRC: "I see no reason for supposing that the [Bell Telephone Laboratories computer] is less broad in scope than the ENIAC. . . . I think the ideal equipment would probably be a combination of relay and electronic devices, but I am very sure that the development time for the electronic equipment would be four to six times as long as that of relay equipment."

In his report to Curtiss three years later, it was clear that there had been little change in Stibitz's position: "I find it difficult to say much about the Mauchly-Eckert proposal. There are so many things undecided that I do not think a contract should be let for the whole job." Stibitz urged a measured development plan, based on the achievement of specific milestones, to be implemented in three stages. Curtiss, however, rejected this approach and adopted a two-phase negotiation plan: First, the launching of a research and study project that, when successfully completed, was to be followed by a second contract for the actual assembly of the system.

Mauchly's high hopes in May 1946 happily bore fruit in June. Curtiss advised Mauchly that if he and Eckert started a company, the National Bureau of Standards was prepared to award them the first of a series of grants that over a period of two years could total as much as $270,000. On the strength of the Curtiss endorsement, Eckert and Mauchly formed a partnership, the Electronic Control Company, and set up shop over a clothing store on Walnut Street in Philadelphia. The first NBS contract, signed on September 25, 1946, authorized payment of $75,000 to their new venture for building scale models of two mercury delay tubes "complete with associated pulse shaping and regenerative circuits" and one magnetic-tape transport system. The delay lines were to be the rapid access memory in a future computer, and the transports would provide the means for writing or reading data in a much larger file stored on magnetic tape.

Because the NBS contract could not support their new company indefinitely, Mauchly began to beat the bushes for other business. One likely prospect surfaced after the passage of new legislation affecting the insurance industry. The Guertin law, which imposed tougher operating standards, including a more complex experience table for the setting of rates, was due to go into effect on January 1, 1948. Compiling the revised tables required a considerable amount of calculations. Consequently, new methods and equipment that might get the job done faster, with less manpower, were very much sought after by the insurance companies.

During a brief tour of navy duty, Edmund C. Berkeley,

an actuary and chief research consultant for the Prudential Insurance Company, had been a member of Howard Aiken's computer group at Harvard University. Soon after returning to Prudential in April 1946, Berkeley was asked to organize a program that would help his company comply with the requirements mandated by the Guertin law. He considered but then rejected the possibility of calculating some of the rates on Aiken's Mark I at Harvard. Then he looked into a new development at IBM, an electronic sequence-controlled calculator, but a more attractive alternative was offered by the Electronic Control Company.

A new input-output technique that Eckert and Mauchly had been hawking along with their other computer ideas promised to be a much faster way to store and retrieve large volumes of data than was possible using traditional punched-card machines. The improvement was made possible by a finding in their recent research that showed that up to 100 alphanumeric characters could be recorded on an inch of metal tape as tiny magnetized bits. The tape, when mounted on reels, could be driven past read-write heads as fast as ninety inches per second. In this way information could be moved from one file to another at the rate of more than a half million characters per minute.

Berkeley, intrigued by the high-speed potential of tape drives, tried to persuade Eckert and Mauchly to build some for Prudential. But the inventors were not willing to sell only a piece of the pie; they wanted Prudential to buy all of it. Magnetic-tape drives, after all, were only one element, albeit an important one, in their proposed general-purpose computer system. Mauchly wrote a letter to Berkeley, dated March 28, 1947, in which he touted the benefits of high-speed arithmetic processing: "It may be that you are not yet convinced that [high processing speeds are] essential for the type of work which you expect to do. However, in our studies of operations in other companies as well as the Census Bureau, we have always found that high internal speed of operation can be translated into reduced cost of operation."

Mauchly was unnecessarily concerned because Berkeley eventually proved to be a powerful ally in selling Prudential's management on the efficacies of electronic computing. But despite Berkeley's help, Mauchly was unable to get any commitment for a complete system. Doubtful about Eckert and Mauchly's financial stability, Prudential declined to sign an order. Instead, the company offered to advance funds for developing magnetic-tape and storage devices in exchange for an option to buy a computer at a later date. Eckert and Mauchly reluctantly agreed to this arrangement, seeing that part of a loaf was better than none.

An earlier prospect, the A. C. Nielsen Company, had similar misgivings about the limited fiscal resources of the Eckert-Mauchly venture. The Chicago-based consumer research company's involvement with the two inventors was initiated by the founder's son, Arthur C. Nielsen, Jr. Late in 1945 the younger Nielsen, then a major in the U.S. Army Corps of Engineers, was assigned to oversee the erection of a new building at the Aberdeen Proving Ground. When completed, it would house ENIAC, which was scheduled to be dismantled and shipped from the Moore School a year later. Nielsen, who got to know Eckert and Mauchly early in the planning stages for the new building and was intrigued by their ideas for commercial successors to ENIAC, proposed using one in his father's market research business. Mauchly, at first, was cool to the suggestion, pointing out that electronic computers were best suited for applications that required large numbers of calculations, such as scientific and engineering problems or compiling government statistics. Nielsen then countered: "Well, [a computer] adds, multiplies and divides and that's what our company does."

Possibly Mauchly's unfamiliarity with the fact that competent consumer research, at that time, was based on massive amounts of arithmetic operations may have prompted his doubts about the need for a computer in Nielsen's business. But the doubts were quickly dispelled when he learned that the Nielsen Company was spending several hundred thousand dollars a year for the rental of IBM punched-card machines to determine the market shares of a brand of toothpaste or a new bar of soap.

Mauchly reversed his position and went after this new prospect. Early in January 1947 he and Eckert offered to sell the Nielsen Company a general-purpose system, including a key-to-tape recorder and a printer, all to be built and delivered within twelve months. The asking price was $100,000. But now there was some foot dragging in the Nielsen camp. More questions were asked. What assurances were there that the balance sheet of the underfinanced Electronic Control Company would improve? Were the technological innovations being proposed really workable? Obviously, Nielsen was not ready to buy. Instead, on February 13, 1947, the two companies entered into an agreement authorizing payment of a modest monthly subsidy to Eckert and Mauchly to help support development work. In exchange, the Nielsen Company was granted an option to buy a computer at some future date.

Meanwhile the cost of doing business skyrocketed. There was a growing payroll to meet, rent to be paid, materials to purchase. The initial $75,000 installment from the National Bureau of Standards was dwindling fast, and no additional payments would be forthcoming until the mercury delay tubes and magnetic-tape transports had been assembled and passed acceptance tests. Hampered by its precarious financial situation and a sales campaign dead in the water, the Electronic Control Company was dealt another blow by a publicity coup on March 2, 1947.

On that date, the wraps were removed from EDVAC, a computer into which had been built many of the design ideas proposed by Eckert and Mauchly prior to their departure from the Moore School a year earlier. At a University of Pennsylvania press conference announcing EDVAC and heralding the advent of a "mercury memory tank," Eckert and Mauchly were not identified as key members of the research team responsible for this achievement. On the following day, the first paragraph of a news feature in the *New York Times* trumpeted: "A new electronic super-calculator, said to be capable of making the Army's world-famous ENIAC look like a dunce, is under construction at the University of Pennsylvania."

Suddenly cast in the role of playing catch-up, Mauchly and his associates hastily organized a response that was covered four days later in an inside page of the *Philadelphia Bulletin:* "Close on the heels of the announcement of EDVAC. . . [Mauchly and Eckert] of the Electronic Control Company announced that they were developing EDVAC II for the U.S. Bureau of the Census."

But no matter what claims were advanced, the record clearly showed that the University of Pennsylvania was the first to announce what Mauchly had been referring to all along as an "EDVAC-like machine." In a long memo to the Electronic Control Company engineering staff on April 3, 1947, Mauchly wrote: "From time to time, it has been suggested that we could find a better name for our machines, but no such name has been [selected]. . . . We cannot postpone this decision longer without loss. . . . If we are going to turn our backs on the word EDVAC, we have got to do it right now and turn up another name to push instead." Then in a tongue-in-cheek move to stimulate thinking about alternate names, Mauchly closed with a question: "Does anyone like the name INFAC—Indiscreet Numerical Fudger and Computer?"

After much chin scratching, someone suggested that they try to find a good synonym for *general purpose*, the term Mauchly frequently used to describe EDVAC's broad range of uses. Why not *Universal?* A Universal Automatic Computer. Here was a name that was not only descriptive but also had a professional ring to it. And so, in a memo dated May 24, 1947, Mauchly decreed that henceforth the major product of the Electronic Control Company would be known as the *Univ*ersal *A*utomatic *C*omputer, or UNIVAC.

In April 1946 Eckert and Mauchly had backed away from Bryan Field's betting machine problem because solving it would have seriously delayed their plans to get into the commercial computer business. A year later, however, while engaged in a desperate struggle to remain solvent, another special project opportunity came along, and this time they seized it. In April 1947 Mauchly was retained as a consultant by Northrop Aircraft, Inc., of Hawthorne, California. Northrop, then deeply immersed in development work on a new missile for the navy, sought Mauchly's advice about the use of digital electronic techniques in the vehicle's guidance system. Mauchly was sufficiently persuasive to convince Northrop management that an electronic digital system could indeed do the job and that the Electronic Control Company was uniquely equipped to build it for them.

Consequently, only six months after being retained as a consultant, Mauchly was awarded a much juicier plum by Northrop. On October 7, 1947, the aerospace manufacturer agreed to pay the cash-starved Electronic Control Company the sum of $100,000 to design and build the prototype of a new airborne computer, later identified as BINAC (*Bin*ary *A*utomatic *C*omputer). The contract authorized monthly payments up to a maximum of $80,000 with the remainder to be paid when BINAC was completed and ready for delivery to Northrop in May 1948.

With this infusion of new cash, the Electronic Control Company narrowly managed to stave off bankruptcy. For a while, at least, there would be no more checkless paydays. But solvency could not make life less complicated. Winning the Northrop contract meant another ball to keep in the air. More staff had to be hired, and Curtiss was growing anxious about the failure to meet demonstration deadlines for the Census Bureau. The Nielsen Company was also becoming restive because there was little to show for the development funds it had advanced, and Mauchly, in a desperate bid for the Northrop business, had agreed to an impossible time schedule: Design, construct, and deliver the prototype of a new airborne computer within six months.

Meanwhile, for Dr. Frank Aydelotte, the scholarly director of the Institute for Advanced Study, there seemed to be no end to the minor but nevertheless annoying administrative problems being generated by von Neumann's computer project. First there was the matter of space. More than six months after the institute's trustees had officially sanctioned von Neumann's plan, the question of where to put the workers had not been answered. In a memo to von Neumann on June 4, 1946, Aydelotte wrote: "I have thought very carefully over the problem of disposing of those fifteen workers who are to arrive the middle of June. The only useable space in our basement is that adjoining the men's lavatory, to which you are most heartily welcome. Aside from that, the only additional room in the building would be the lecture room and possibly the Mathematics Library, both of which I know you would be reluctant to use. . . . I have thought of various other expedients. If we could get a Quonset hut, I should be glad to erect it in one of the parking lots, allowing it to remain there for four or five months. There is a certain amount of space in the second, third, and fourth storey halls of the Institute which could be occupied by desk workers, although these are not suitable for laboratory purposes."

A year later Aydelotte, still burdened by mundane administrative matters and concerned that the computer project was corrupting the pristine intellectual environment of the institute, wrote plaintively on June 10, 1947, to von Neumann: "I have approved salt tablets, electric fans and the loan to [a project employee] with some misgivings in each case. Will you undertake in accordance with our conversation [to tell him that] we consider him still to be on trial and that we do not assure him of his position beyond December 31, 1947? . . . I am a little disturbed about the whole question of order and discipline in the computer project and am afraid that the atmosphere is a little bit injured by its proximity to the Institute. Insofar as the computer project partakes [as you say] of the nature of an industrial operation it should, of course, be run on industrial lines. Insofar as it is a research project, the methods of the Institute are applicable. I can see the difficulties which you face in assimilating these two points of view."

That same month, while von Neumann was assuring Aydelotte that the computer project was enhancing rather than hindering the academic pursuits of the institute, Konrad Zuse, viewing his own future, was convinced that prospects could hardly be worse. Three of his computers, the Z1, Z2, and Z3, lay buried in the bomb rubble of Berlin. Stripped of his resources, without staff or funds, and holed up in a small mountain village in southern Germany, Zuse was figuratively and geographically isolated from the mainstream of computer development.

Six years earlier, shortly after the abortive meeting with the German intelligence officer, Zuse had been inducted into the army but soon discharged on grounds that his skill as an engineer was more valuable to the German Reich than his prowess as a soldier. He was assigned to work in the engineering department of Henschel Flugzeugwerken, A.G., Berlin. At that time Henschel was manufacturing V2 rockets, which the Germans later launched against England from occupied France. Part of the test procedure at Henschel involved measurement and readjustment of wing angles so that each missile coming off the production line would conform, when launched, to a predetermined flight pattern. This process required the services of dozens of mathematicians who pounded out computations day and night on a battery of mechanical calculators. The calculators were not designed for round-the-clock operations and broke down frequently, causing many assembly line delays.

After observing these recurring slowdowns, Zuse went to his superior and explained how he could build a computer that would do all of this calculating much better and faster. Zuse immediately had his undivided attention. Parts were requisitioned, workers were assigned to this new project, and Zuse started to construct a machine, which on completion in early 1942, was identified as the S1. Every day thereafter for the next two years, the S1 clacked through some 800 computations per rocket, which, with the mechanical calculators out of the picture, rolled off Henschel's production line at the rate of one every ten minutes.

Zuse's triumph with the S1 in 1942 rekindled official interest in the Z series, and he was relieved of his regular duties to work full time on the development of general-purpose computers. This enabled him to finish his Z2 and go on to build a Z3 and a Z4. However, the landing of Anglo-American forces in Normandy in June 1944 and the subsequent capture of the V2 launching sites in northern France and Holland rendered the rocket program useless.

Early in 1945, as Allied and Russian armies drove relentlessly toward Berlin in a giant pincer movement, orders were finally issued to stop production at Henschel, strip the factory of machinery, and move everything out. Zuse was allocated limited transport (one truck) on which he loaded his Z4. His earlier computers were left behind. Then, in the last days of the war, Zuse and a few colleagues joined a convoy moving south. Zuse eventually wound up in a small village in the Alps, alone, but still in possession of his Z4, which had been hidden in the cellar of the house where he then lived.

Rumors began to circulate about the mysterious contraption that Zuse had brought with him, and the villagers, fearful that it would explode and kill them all, frantically sought aid from the Allies. Two intelligence officers were dispatched to interview Zuse and look at his machine. Zuse welcomed this visit because he realized that he needed the help of those now in power to sanction and support his future work in computing. His hopes were dashed, however, when at the end of the interview one of his visitors turned to the other and said: "It's only a calculator . . . it's of no interest to us."

In the summer of 1947, however, Zuse's luck changed for the better. One of Zuse's friends, as a result of his marriage to an American woman, was exempt from the restrictions concerning travel by Germans to the United States. During a trip to America, he managed to gain an audience with Thomas J. Watson, Sr., president of IBM. "Mr. Watson," he said, "you are in the calculator business. You ought to see the advanced calculator that my friend Zuse has back in Germany."

Watson contacted representatives of the Hollerith Company, which before the war had been affiliated with IBM operations, and asked them to see Zuse. They did and reported back that Zuse had proposed several ideas that IBM could profitably adapt. Shortly thereafter, Zuse was under contract to IBM. But this arrangement did not rule out a subsequent association with Remington Rand, another American calculator manufacturer. That company provided the backing for Zuse to start a business in Essen, West Germany, which eventually installed many relay computers throughout Europe. Zuse was on his way again.

CHAPTER 9

Hail Britannia!

Professor Douglas R. Hartree unbuckled his seat belt as the Pan American Airways flight from London rolled to a stop before a passenger gate at La Guardia Airport in New York. His arrival on this Easter Sunday morning in 1946 signaled the start of a concerted effort to develop new research projects for ENIAC. Hartree, one of England's most distinguished mathematical physicists, had come to the United States to spearhead this work in response to a request by the U.S. Army's chief of ordnance.

The previous summer, Hartree had visited the Moore School briefly during a tour of American computational centers that had been organized by the British Commonwealth Scientific Office. Now he had come back to serve for three months as an expert adviser. Col. Paul Gillon, in a letter from the Pentagon to the commanding general of the Aberdeen Proving Ground, noted that the ordnance command was indeed fortunate in obtaining Hartree's services and wrote: "Now that the overwhelming urgency of conventional computations has abated, it is exceedingly important that the Ballistic Research Laboratory, which possesses perhaps the largest and best equipped computing organization in the world, strive to distinguish itself in the pioneer character of computational work. Since Professor Hartree has always been one of the outstanding leaders in the exploration of new problems by computing devices, it is believed that his presence should be stimulating to the Laboratory staff in exploring the possibilities of the ENIAC relative to the research programs of the Laboratory."

After spending a few days in Washington being briefed by Colonel Gillon and consulting with ordnance department officials, Hartree went to Philadelphia to begin his work at the Moore School. His first month was largely given over to a meticulous analysis of ENIAC's design, including lengthy discussions with the Moore School project teams. During the second and third months he gained some "hands on" experience with ENIAC by continuing work on a problem he had started to solve before his departure from England. In a preliminary report submitted at the end of his three-month assignment, Hartree, alluding to the running of his problem on an electronic computer, wrote: "The experience was . . . the most exhilarating piece of research I have done for many years."

But the main thrust of the report was an expression of concern about the current staff and proposed relocation of ENIAC to Aberdeen. While acknowledging that at least four members of the ENIAC staff were highly skilled in operating it, "none of them has the width of mathematical knowledge and research experience necessary to organize the work, devise new methods for handling problems, and generally give the work a research character when required." Hartree was convinced that the appointment of someone endowed with vigor and a "breadth of knowledge" was the most important step that could be taken to ensure full use of ENIAC's extraordinary computing power.

Hartree was equally alarmed by the probability that ENIAC would be rendered useless for many months while it was being moved from the Moore School to its intended permanent site in Aberdeen. He had reason to be concerned. Earlier during his visit, ENIAC was shut down one night in response to a public appeal by the local power company, which wanted to conserve dwindling fuel supplies resulting from a coal strike. The aftermath of that move was disastrous. When power was restored the next day, troubles blossomed like dandelions on a warm day in May. Many circuit components, unable to handle the sudden onslaught of current after hours of inactivity, sputtered and expired. Others, pushed to the borderline, vacillated between operating and subnormal modes. And invisible hairline cracks in some soldered junctions that had presented no problem before the power was cut off were now blocking pulses one second and conducting them the next. Locating the causes of these transient failures was difficult and time consuming because there could be no certainty that an intermittent had been found and eliminated until the circuit worked flawlessly for at least two or three days.

Coping with just a few transient failures was a tricky business. But when dozens cropped up at the same time, picking one's way through the maze of errant circuits was mind boggling. Hartree therefore warned: "I fear much more trouble from the move to Aberdeen, and would not willingly accept the chance of it if there were prospects of leaving ENIAC where it is, at least until another machine is developed, so that something would be working while ENIAC is out of action."

From the standpoint of those who might reap benefits from its use, Hartree had a point. If ENIAC was kept on station in the Moore School until EDVAC was completed, there would be no hiatus in high-speed computing. To do otherwise meant that every scientist now waiting to run his problem on an electronic computer would suffer the same fate as a child who having been offered a bag of succulent gumdrops now saw them snatched away.

But following Hartree's advice was easier said than done. The departures months earlier of Eckert, Mauchly, and other members of the original ENIAC team had seriously slowed progress of the successor machine, and at the time Hartree wrote his report no one could guarantee that EDVAC would be completed within two years. Nor was anyone willing to step forward and tell the army to postpone its plans to install ENIAC in Aberdeen until some unspecified date in the future.

Hartree, of course, was a realist and concluded his references to the matter with a final comment: "I am sure that there are other considerations involved, but since I have been asked to give my views freely, and regard this matter of some importance, I am expressing them. . . . If ENIAC is moved, I think it should be done with all possible precautions, as if it were an explosive which might go off with some minor jarring or vibration."

Shortly after completing his report, Hartree returned to England where, with evangelical fervor, he set out to spread the good news about ENIAC. He had been unable to speak publicly about it after a government-sanctioned visit to the Moore School in July 1945 because the project was still under security wraps. Now he was no longer bound by such constraints. He quickly established himself as one of England's leading authorities on electronic computing by writing a detailed description of ENIAC for publication in the October 12, 1946, issue of *Nature*, the prestigious scientific journal. While enthusiastically promoting the concept of computing with electronics, Hartree was also very much the dedicated scientist, eschewing any tendency to go off the deep end. He vigorously challenged anyone who ascribed more powers than deserved to this astonishing computing tool, and his determination to keep the record straight prompted him to take on a member of the royal family itself.

The occasion was the twenty-first anniversary of the founding of the British Institution of Engineers, which was celebrated at a dinner in the Savoy Hotel in London on October 31, 1946. Admiral Lord Mountbatten of Burma, the principal speaker, in acknowledging the rapid developments in the realm of electronics during World War II, alluded to "the most Wellsian of them all," the ENIAC. The following day, the *Times* (London) reported Mountbatten's reference to an "electronic brain which would perform functions analogous to those at present undertaken by the semi-automatic portions of the human brain." Mountbatten also predicted that machines would soon be in use that would "exercise a degree of memory, while some were being designed to employ those hitherto human prerogatives of choice and judgment."

In a letter published in the *Times* a few days later, Hartree deprecated Mountbatten's "use of the term 'electronic brain' as a descriptive title of ENIAC and other machines." Hartree maintained that computing machines do only precisely what they are instructed to do by the operators who set them up. While agreeing that computing circuits exercise a certain degree of judgment, he cautioned," It must be clearly understood that the situation in which judgment is exercised, the criteria to be applied, the way the results of applying these criteria are to be assessed, and the decisions as to the action to be taken on these results, must be fully thought out and anticipated in setting up the machines." In other words, concluded Hartree, "Use of the machine is no substitute for the thought of organizing the computations, only for the labour in carrying them out. It seems to me that the distinction is important and that the term 'electronic brain' obscures it and is misleading. . . . This is why I hope use of this term will be avoided in the future."

In a few short months, Hartree, through publication of

the ENIAC paper in *Nature* and the widely circulated rebuttal to Lord Mountbatten's address, had firmly established himself as one of England's early champions of electronic computing. But his was not his only claim to fame. Computing, in Hartree's view, as it was originally to John Mauchly, was merely a means to an end. Mauchly, for example, would not have started tinkering with gas-tube logic circuits if he had found another way to analyze the vast store of meteorological data buried in the archives of the Carnegie Institution in Washington, D.C. Nor would Hartree have expended so much time and energy searching for more efficient ways to handle and process data during the early 1940s if the nature of his work had not impelled him to do so.

Hartree was a distinguished mathematical physicist who had made major scientific contributions in the field of crystal structure analysis. When physicists at the time referred to "S" values (the structural factor that governs the configurations of electrons in the atoms of a molecule), they were citing findings that were derived from what was known as "Hartree's self-consistent fields."

During the early 1940s, crystal structure analysis was the vehicle that enabled Hartree to identify and begin dialogs with other scientists who had a yen for dabbling in computing. One was Andrew W. Booth, who, during World War II, headed a government study project at the University of Birmingham that explored the crystal structure of explosives. Booth's duties included overseeing several young women whose task it was to perform numerous arithmetic operations with data compiled during experiments. It was repetitive and mind-numbing work, and Booth, sympathetic to their plight, tried to lessen the monotony by tightening up the mathematical procedures as well as designing and building some small hand calculators.

At the end of the war, Booth decided that if he succeeded in finding another crystalographic assignment, he would certainly do something about the tiresome calculations that were the unavoidable consequence of such research. Subsequent appointments to a post in the British Rubber Producers Association and a lectureship at Birbeck College provided Booth with the resources and the opportunity to start building computing machines to attack crystalographic problems.

Word of this activity soon reached Hartree, who wrote to the British Rubber Producers Association asking what Booth was doing as well as requesting permission to visit its laboratories in order to meet him. When Hartree came, Booth was working on a Fourier synthesizing device. An early first attempt had been purely mechanical, but in succeeding models Booth had been applying digital computation techniques. When Hartree saw them, he told Booth about the electronic computing projects at the Moore School in Philadelphia and the Institute for Advanced Study.

Pursuing Hartree's tip, Booth subsequently secured funding for a year's stay (1946–47) at the Institute for Advanced Study, working with the von Neumann team. When he returned to England, Booth drew upon his experience in Princeton to build a series of machines, the APECs (All *Pur*-pose *E*lectronic *C*omputers). However, the flow of computer know-how between England and America was by no means only in one direction. During the late 1940s, there were several significant developments in Britain that were later adopted in American computer programs.

CHAPTER 10

Growing Pains

By plucking Eckert and Mauchly's Electronic Control Company from the brink of bankruptcy in October 1947, Northrop Aircraft Corporation simultaneously became a welcome rescuer and a troublesome taskmaster. Immediately after issuing its $100,000 contract for BINAC, Northrop, sensing that Eckert and Mauchly's preoccupation with general-purpose computer development might drain resources away from the guided missile project, took steps to consolidate its position.

From the perspective of a large corporation with precisely and carefully planned business strategies, the small firm in Philadelphia was veering wildly out of control. Consequently, Eckert and Mauchly were persuaded to ask Gene M. Clute, a member of Northrop's management team, to come in and tighten things up. Shortly after his arrival on the scene, Clute concluded that his efforts should be directed to the achievement of two objectives: One, make the Electronic Control Company more attractive to potential investors, and two, create an environment that projects an image of stability to customers and prospects.

As a partnership, with Eckert and Mauchly owning equal shares, the Electronic Control Company seemed the ideal vehicle for two young men starting out in business, but with nearly forty people on the payroll and negotiations under way with various agencies of the U.S. government and at least a dozen other prospects, it was far too rudimentary an arrangement. Clute, therefore, set the wheels in motion to incorporate. On December 22, 1947, Eckert and Mauchly signed over their assets in the partnership to the Eckert-Mauchly Computer Corporation. Accepting for this new business entity were John Mauchly, its president, and Gene M. Clute, secretary. Under the terms of the agreement, 15,000 shares of stock were authorized at a par value of $1.00 per share. Eckert, vice president of the new corporation, and Mauchly each received 6,750 shares and 1,500 shares were retained as treasury stock.

The delivery of a letter from Northrop's assistant general counsel, George Gore, in October 1947, that notified Mauchly that he had been awarded a $100,000 order should have propelled the new company forward into a new phase of growth. But four months later little progress had been made, and Mauchly complained bitterly to Clute and Eckert in a memo dated February 5, 1948: "The more I think about the situation in which we find ourselves at present, the more I am convinced that we are losing a hell of a lot of valuable time [because] we are slow in making necessary decisions."

There was one decision, however, that had been made quickly and about which there was no argument: More stock must be sold to raise more capital. But there was considerable hemming and hawing when it came to the matter of choosing the best time to issue new stock. Mauchly was agitated by the lack of consensus on this point, which was forcing the deferral of many other decisions because no money was available to implement them.

It was a classic business dilemma. Rushing out quickly with a new stock issue might attract less capital than would be gained by waiting until more orders were on the books; more orders would make the venture more interesting to potential investors and help boost the selling price per share. But deals that Mauchly forecast would be closed soon would not be closed until prospects could be shown that the Eckert-Mauchly Computer Corporation had, in fact, acquired more financing.

Mauchly saw a way to avoid this problem by wooing the American Research and Development Corporation, a group of Boston investors specializing in small companies with proven growth potential, and the A. C. Nielsen Company, the Chicago-based market research firm. American Research and Development appeared to be a particularly good fit. It had $5 million, which its charter specified was to be invested in new high-technology enterprises with a maximum of 10 percent of the total capitalization going to any single company. When Mauchly learned about American Research and Development, it had no more than four or five client companies, which meant that half, possibly more, of its total capital remained uncommitted. The A. C. Nielsen Company, a major prospect for a UNIVAC system, was also considered a likely investor. Mauchly believed this because he knew that Nielsen was then paying several hundred thousand dollars per year for the rental of punched-card machines. Keeping the computer company afloat was very much in Nielsen's interests, Mauchly reasoned, because replacing the rental equipment with a UNIVAC would save a bundle in operating costs.

Mauchly also knew that the deal would be more palatable if the price was right. In his February 5 memo to Clute and Eckert, Mauchly also said, "To get the interest and cooperation of these organizations, and to resolve the financial questions quickly, I think we can afford to set a price which might be under that which we could obtain if we held out and haggled and bargained for a considerable period." The price Mauchly had in mind was $40 per share. When the corporation was formed in December 1947, its charter authorized the issuance of 15,000 shares of stock. If the number of authorized shares was increased to 25,000 and 6,000 were sold, proposed Mauchly, a cash infusion of $240,000 would be realized. But this was not to be. American Research and Development declined Mauchly's overtures, and the A. C. Nielsen Company, which earlier had dickered unsuccessfully for a majority interest in the Eckert-Mauchly venture, decided to limit its involvement to the monthly subsidy for work then in progress.

Meanwhile, relations with other customers continued to deteriorate. John H. Curtiss, the National Bureau of Standards bureaucrat who monitored Eckert and Mauchly's dealings with several government agencies, was fretting about delays and missed deadlines. But what worried Curtiss most was the company's perilous financial condition. Mauchly cited this discontent to support his belief that a massive campaign should be launched immediately to find suitable investors. He contended that if they were well financed, Curtiss would be disposed to give them more machine contracts. Mauchly felt that Curtiss was afraid they would go broke, but the more orders Curtiss gave them, the worse it would be if they failed.

Disenchantment with the Eckert-Mauchly Computer Corporation seemed to be spreading like a plague. While worries about that company's cash flow problems were no minor concern, Northrop Aircraft was growing increasingly restive about its Philadelphia subcontractor for other reasons. One was that three months before the scheduled completion of BINAC in May 1948, John Mauchly warned Northrop about the first of several delivery-date postponements. The second was Mauchly's discovery that his company could not live with the $100,000 figure specified in the contract. Costs for design, construction, and system tests had escalated well beyond original estimates, and there was no doubt that the price was far too low. Northrop management's dismay about the delivery-date slippages was exacerbated by Mauchly's persistent pleas for more money.

Northrop was having second thoughts. Its decision to order a BINAC, which in a sense was a vote of no confidence in its own professional staff, may have been a mistake. Early in 1946, Erik Ackerlund, the missile project manager for Northrop, had hired Floyd George Steele, the first of several electronic engineers to come aboard to work on a computer for the guidance system. Steele was soon joined by another engineer, Richard E. Sprague. The development group grew quickly thereafter, and by January 1947—nearly ten months before the BINAC agreement with Mauchly—Northrop's own computer team had produced a digital differential analyzer (DIDA) and was well on the way to completion of a successor machine incorporating more advanced computer technology.

The announcement by Northrop's management that outsiders had been engaged to build a guidance computer for the new missile came as a bolt from the blue for Steele and his group. After the initial shock wore off, they dismissed this affront to their professional pride and, in the words of Richard Sprague: "swallowed our resentment and accepted the assignment of liaison engineers with the [Eckert-Mauchly] company." But while subsequent problems with Eckert-Mauchly's progress prompted some in Northrop's management to press for cancellation of the BINAC contract and recommend revitalizing Northrop's own computer operations, nothing came of it. Too much water had gone over the dam.

Mauchly's search for a financial backer who could breathe new life into his cash-starved company bore fruit in the summer of 1948. Howard Aiken's comment, two years earlier, that there was a lot of money to be made at the racetracks, had made little sense to Eckert and Mauchly at the time, but now it did. For it was the president of American Totalisator Company, the manufacturer of the pari-mutuel odds-making machines that Bryan Field had sought to displace from Delaware Park, who came to their rescue. Introduced to Mauchly by a mutual friend, Henry L. Straus quickly saw that buying a substantial interest in the troubled computer company would accomplish two things. First, a potentially dangerous competitor, who might possibly build a betting machine superior to the ones made by American Totalisator, would be brought into the fold. Second, Straus and his firm would have access to the electronics expertise of the Eckert-Mauchly company as well as share in its future growth.

Straus and Mauchly might never have met, nor indeed would Straus have been likely to go into the totalisator business, had it not been for Cockney, an obscure, second-rate horse. One afternoon, during the 1927 spring meeting at Havre de Grace, Maryland, Straus and his party cheered Cockney on as the field moved into the home stretch. Cockney, though not a favorite, and therefore listed on the probable odds boards at nine to one, was nevertheless a "hot tip" that Straus and his friends had picked to win. As Cockney crossed the finish line, they congratulated each other and headed for the payoff windows. But betting on Cockney had been heavier than anticipated and, after a ten-minute delay, the official payoff was posted as $7.20 for a $2.00 bet. A great howl arose from the crowd. Later, a friend of Straus, who had wagered $10.00 and received $36.00 instead of the $100.00 he had expected, turned to him and said: "You're an engineer. Why don't you invent a machine that will give accurate odds? Not just once in a while but all the time, as the betting is going on. Then we would know where we stand."

Straus, who was no less annoyed by the inaccurate betting odds reports, promptly accepted the challenge. A few months later he took some of his ideas to the General Electric Company. Executives there were reluctant to collaborate with him because they did not want to be associated with a gambling device, but one vice president, John Upp, was a racing buff and took the Straus project under his wing. Arthur J. Johnston of General Electric's Remote Control Division was assigned to work with Straus, and together they built a machine comprised of electric relays and rotary switches. It was demonstrated to the owners of several American racetracks in the summer of 1928. Everyone who saw it was impressed. But no one had enough confidence to step forward and be the first to order one.

Straus was disheartened and close to abandoning his invention when, in the late fall of 1928, the English parliament legalized pari-mutuel betting at Britain's racetracks. As a result, a new, ready-made market for the Johnson-Straus totalisator was created, and Straus hastened to exploit it. In February 1929 a model of his machine was successfully demonstrated for the British Racecourse Betting Control Board, and a year later the first installation was made at Thirsk. Additional systems were acquired by other English tracks, and Straus thought the time had come to duplicate these successes in America.

But track owners in the United States did not warm to the Straus invention as quickly as their English cousins and, during 1930 and 1931, sales by Straus were limited to supplying electric odds and payoff boards to Pimlico, Bowie, Empire City, and Hialeah. The totalisator concept, however, was by no means ahead of its time in America. One made by another manufacturer was imported from Australia by Charles A. and Gurnee Munn of Palm Beach for the 1931 Hialeah meeting. Its debut was a disaster because it broke down frequently and the errors it generated were maddeningly difficult to trace. In desperation the Munns turned for help to Straus, who was able to iron out the bugs in time for the 1932 meeting, which, from the standpoint of pari-mutuel operations, went smoothly. By October 1932 the Munns were sufficiently impressed by Straus and his invention to enter into an agreement with him to form the American Totalisator Company, which set up headquarters in Baltimore, Maryland.

The company flourished, and by the time Straus encountered John Mauchly in 1948, Straus had amassed considerable wealth and was frequently identified in the columns of Baltimore newspapers as a nationally prominent sportsman. The immensely profitable totalisator business, coupled with other investments and various racetrack interests, equipped Straus for a life of gentlemanly leisure, which centered around hunting and breeding thoroughbreds at Leyland, a large estate in Maryland that he had purchased from Alfred Gwynne Vanderbilt. But Straus never overcame the compulsion to take on new challenges. A vigorous fifty-three years old when he came upon the struggling young computer company in Philadelphia, Straus, an electrical engineer by profession and the developer of an odds-making system in use at every major racetrack in America and England, was better prepared to assess the potential of the Eckert-Mauchly venture than most other investors.

Before Straus arrived on the scene, Mauchly, while desperately courting potential backers, was continually rejecting offers that would require the two inventors to relinquish majority ownership of their company. The deal proposed by Straus, however, would not. Straus persuaded the Munns and other directors of American Totalisator to provide the Eckert-Mauchly Computer Corporation with the operating cash it needed by accepting a series of notes over a period of eighteen months. At predetermined intervals, the notes that were held by American Totalisator would be exchanged for Eckert-Mauchly shares until, by the termination of the agreement, the computer company would have been strengthened by $400,000 in cash and American

Totalisator would own 40 percent of Eckert-Mauchly's authorized stock.

While Straus was willing to leave majority ownership in the hands of Eckert and Mauchly, he was nevertheless sufficiently cautious to want the power of a veto over any rash moves they might propose. Under the provisions of the computer company's charter, however, the shares controlled by American Totalisator could gain no more than one seat on the three-member Eckert-Mauchly board. To satisfy the Straus requirement that no major decisions could be made without his concurrence, the number of board members was increased in two phases. The first, authorized at a regular meeting of the Eckert-Mauchly board on June 15, 1948, created two additional board seats. Until then, the board was composed of Eckert, Mauchly, and the man proposed by Northrop Aircraft, Gene M. Clute. The two new vacancies were filled by George V. Eltgroth, who had joined the company six months earlier as general counsel, and T. Wistar Brown, a star IBM salesman who had just joined the company as sales manager.

The second increase, from five to nine directors, was voted in a special meeting of the board on August 6, 1948. The four additional seats would be occupied by candidates representing shares owned by American Totalisator: Henry L. Straus; Harold Robinson, another AmTote executive; and Charles A. and Gurnee Munn who, with Straus, were major shareholders in the Baltimore-based company.

The expansion of the board was a necessary preliminary step in the process but did not empower Straus to block any major project if, in his view, it would be inimical to the best interests of AmTote. The agreement entered into by the two companies also specified that, for certain matters, the Eckert-Mauchly charter would be amended to require approval of two-thirds of the board (six members) instead of a simple majority. Actions to be governed by this ruling included any salary increases over the $6,000-per-year level, payment of bonuses, setting up pension or profit-sharing plans, capital expenditures in excess of $1,000 per item, negotiating for the acquisition of property, and the signing of any contract whose estimated cost of performance would exceed $50,000.

When the last signature was inked on the agreement, Eckert and Mauchly retained a majority interest in their company but could do little without the blessing of at least one director representing AmTote's shares. Another condition, shrewdly imposed by Straus, designated AmTote as the exclusive sales agent for any products produced by Eckert-Mauchly "used in connection with horse and dog racing."

After Straus and his associates were formally declared members of the board during a meeting of that body on August 19, 1948, Mauchly, who was presiding, pointed out that another recent amendment to the company's by-laws authorized the seating of a chairman. By prearrangement, Straus was the lone nominee for the post, and after election by unanimous vote, he replaced Mauchly as chairman of the meeting. The only other business was a resolution that instructed the secretary, Gene Clute, to call a meeting of the stockholders to ratify these actions. It was passed quickly and Straus declared the meeting adjourned.

Although the monthly cash loans from American Totalisator would greatly ease the computer company's financial troubles, money alone could not solve another serious problem. Taking on the BINAC project in the summer of 1947 had been a desperation move meant to keep Eckert and Mauchly in business. From the standpoint of their relatively small staff, however, it was a case of biting off more than they could chew. In August 1948 the BINAC, months behind schedule and alarmingly over budget, was draining off an inordinate amount of effort that might have been invested profitably in other ways.

Sensing that they had unwittingly been drawn into a hopeless trap by their commitment to Northrop, Mauchly proposed making the most of a bad situation by going into the BINAC business. Most of the losses incurred in designing a single BINAC for Northrop could be recovered, Mauchly argued, by building more for other customers. But Eckert had doubts. At a meeting of the executive committee on August 24, 1948, Eckert declared that UNIVAC design and production would be set back a month, possibly more, if the engineering department had to modify the BINAC for general-purpose applications. Delay a decision on this matter for another five weeks, Eckert urged, and he could then give a detailed assessment of the probable impact on UNIVAC.

Mauchly, however, wanted to push ahead. In a memo written a few days later to Eckert, Straus, and Clute, he cited a reason why an immediate decision was critically important: "At a meeting to be held September 10th, the University of Illinois is going to consider... purchasing a BINAC or a UNIVAC. If... we tell them that there is no use in considering a BINAC, [they will only have to decide] whether they are able and willing to contract for a UNIVAC.... They are also considering the alternative of attempting to build their own computer.... Since [their funds are limited] and [compared to BINAC] a later delivery and a higher price is quoted for a UNIVAC, it could turn out that with only the UNIVAC to consider, they might prefer to try building their own." Mauchly was defining the choice in terms of dollars and cents: Market the lower-priced BINAC, too, and make more sales sooner, or concentrate only on the more expensive UNIVAC systems and limit the number of potential buyers.

The validity of Mauchly's position would never be determined because he could not rally the support to test it. There would be only one BINAC and, once it was shipped, everyone could get back to the main business at hand—building UNIVACs. But BINAC's problems would not go away. On October 22, 1948, Mauchly dispatched a long letter to Northrop's Frank Bell. First, he offered some good news: BINAC, at last, was in its final testing stage. Then, once again, Mauchly tried to explain the causes of BINAC's frequent delivery postponements and escalating costs. The difficulties, according to Mauchly, stemmed from the fact that there had not been one contractual agreement but two. Mauchly, in referring to the initial agreement of July 27, 1947, said: "Certain specifications were laid down, and it appeared possible to build equipment meeting these specifications for a price not to exceed $100,000, with delivery date May 15, 1948." The second letter, dated October 9, 1947, made a change in the specifications, "but this change was such that it was difficult for us at the time to foresee to what extent the cost or time of delivery would be modified."

Mauchly then claimed that he would have been in a far better position to estimate a new price and construction schedule had the specifications in the July 27 letter been defined in terms of needed memory size or maximum operating times for certain arithmetic operations. But they were not. Nor was any guidance provided concerning a recommended method for solving the problem BINAC was supposed to attack. The reason for the latter omission was that no one knew, at the time, what method to recommend. Instead of clarifying these points, Northrop's letter of October 9th made matters worse. In defending the slipped delivery dates a year later, Mauchly charged that the revised specifications only muddied the waters: "[In the October 9 letter] a new problem, constituting a considerable generalization of the prior one, was substituted for the old one, preserving, however, the same accuracy and time limits. It was apparent that the task set by the new specifications was more difficult than that set by the older specifications. It was, however, impossible at the time to say much more than this, since studies had not yet been made [defining] possible methods of solution."

In order to bring order out of this chaos, several mathematical studies were conducted in parallel with the design and construction of the computing equipment itself. Mauchly reported to Bell that these studies proved "the memory capacity and other facilities of the computing equipment as constructed are adequate for the solution of the problem set by the October 9th specifications, and it is also apparent that the task set by the earlier specifications of July 27th could have been fulfilled by a somewhat smaller and simpler computing device." What this meant, of course, was that the actual cost of building BINAC had climbed much higher than the contract price of $100,000. Mauchly then explained that the additional costs incurred as a result of the October 9 revisions amounted to $30,000. What would Northrop be getting for this 30 percent surcharge? Actually, quite a bit. According to Mauchly, it was "the difference between a pair of computers having a memory capacity of 256 words, which would have been adequate for the earlier specifications, and a memory of 512 words, which is made necessary by the October 9th specifications."

Mauchly's reference to a "pair of computers" meant that BINAC was essentially two identical computers operating as one. These Siamese twins constantly checked each other, step by step, four million times per second, at each beat of an internal electronic clock. When rated against ENIAC, BINAC did far more with much less. While ENIAC, a decimal machine using numerals zero through nine, required 18,000 standard vacuum tubes, BINAC, operating with the much simpler two-digit binary code, needed fewer than 800 miniatures for its two arithmetic processors and associated memories.

Evaluating the technological gains achieved in the successive designs of ENIAC, BINAC, and UNIVAC can be likened to describing the contrast between the sound of the sputtering motor powering the first flights of the Wright Brothers at Kitty Hawk and the roar of the mighty engines on a Cape Canaveral launching pad. Operating specifications tell only part of the story. Internal memory capacity: ENIAC, 200 decimal digits; BINAC, equivalent of 4,500 decimal digits; UNIVAC, 12,000 decimal digits. Input/output speed: ENIAC, 8,000 decimal digits per minute; BINAC, 60,000; UNIVAC, 600,000. Multiplication of two numbers, each made up of ten decimal digits: ENIAC, 18,-000 per minute; BINAC and UNIVAC, 30,000 per minute.

The BINAC could solve twenty linear equations simultaneously in twenty unknowns. UNIVAC would solve hundreds of equations, each dealing in hundreds of unknowns, in the blink of an eye. By any measure, these were phenomenal gains for less than a decade of effort.

CHAPTER 11

BINAC Countdown

Leafing through his Eckert-Mauchly file, George Gore, the Northrop Aircraft general counsel, viewed the record with dismay. The October 9, 1947, contract specified that all work on BINAC would be completed by May 15, 1948. That deadline had not been met, nor had three subsequent extensions, the last of which, authorized by Northrop in October 1948, required that Eckert and Mauchly deliver BINAC, after a series of rigid acceptance tests, no later than January 1, 1949.

In April 1949 assurances were being transmitted from Philadelphia that BINAC would be ready for shipment to Northrop's Hawthorne, California, headquarters on September 1, 1949. In the meantime, to secure objective and current progress reports on the BINAC project, Frank C. Bell, Northrop's manager of the guided missile program, dispatched a deputy, Richard H. Baker, to be his full-time observer in Philadelphia. Baker arrived there the first week in May, and Bell, in a move to allay any anxieties that may have been caused by this arrangement, wrote to Mauchly:

"I want to be sure that you understand Dick Baker's present position. [He is] to be an observer primarily. [However] if you want us to furnish engineering help to work under your supervision on the completion of the machine . . . I shall be very glad to consider such a suggestion. . . . But short of such an arrangement, I don't want Dick Baker to take the responsibility for carrying out any operation required for the completion of BINAC." For the time being, at least, BINAC was still very much Eckert and Mauchly's baby.

Although BINAC was seriously behind schedule, Mauchly nevertheless viewed efforts to hasten its shipment to California with mixed feelings. Because BINAC was considerably closer to completion than the Census Bureau's first UNIVAC, Mauchly managed to persuade John H. Curtiss, the official computer overseer for the federal government, to permit the running of certain tests on BINAC (which Mauchly was now calling the "prototype" of UNIVAC) to satisfy some of the UNIVAC contract conditions and thereby trigger the release of additional funds being held in escrow. But Northrop got wind of this and protested. Testing UNIVAC programs on BINAC, objected Frank Bell, would unnecessarily delay BINAC's testing and subsequent shipment to Hawthorne.

The reason for Bell's hard line on this issue was explained in a report that George Eltgroth sent to Eckert and Mauchly on May 27, 1949: "Mr. Bell stated that BINAC was actually required on the scene at Hawthorne to make certain demonstrations which would satisfy a policy-making body only if that body actually witnessed them. [Therefore] any arrangements for a protracted stay of the BINAC [in Philadelphia] is foreclosed."

On June 12, 1949, with BINAC's delivery deadline less than ten weeks away, Richard Baker's letter to Frank Bell indicated that much work remained to be done: "During the last week, the BINAC has operated as a complete machine approximately one hour. This is with certain limitations of course. . . . Only one quarter of the second memory is operating. . . . The channels of the first memory are inoperative and the others will need re-alignment soon. . . . Alignment of the second memory has begun, but of the first five channels tried, only four could be made operative. . . . The function of reading from the memory to the tape is inoperative."

Baker also wrote that he had an off-the-record discussion with Joseph Weiner, the Eckert-Mauchly chief engineer. Baker advised Weiner in an indirect way that Weiner "should either devote more of his time to the BINAC or none at all." Apparently Weiner took this criticism well because, according to Baker, Weiner was more cooperative in his dealings with Baker after the conversation.

Baker's presence in Philadelphia also enabled him to transmit some intelligence that must have rankled Bell: "Eckert and Mauchly intend to solve certain design problems for the UNIVAC on the BINAC. Coding of these problems is in progress. I do not know if there is any objection on the part of Eckert-Mauchly in our knowing this, since I discovered it accidentally."

Having Baker constantly looking over their shoulders was one thing, but the prospect of more Northrop people poking around the BINAC assembly area created new tensions. In order to familiarize some Northrop personnel with BINAC's design, Bell decided to send a team of five engineers to Philadelphia to start learning how to use it. When Weiner heard that they were coming, he confronted Baker and told him that "not one of the five men expected to be sent will be allowed to touch the machine" until he, Weiner, is released from responsibility for it.

The cadre from Northrop, however, would spend most of its time in a classroom, which was another complication. Completing BINAC and moving it through the prescribed checkpoints before the September 1 deadline was demanding most of Eckert and Mauchly's attention. Therefore, organizing an instruction course, considered a second-order priority, was a task for which neither was prepared. In a letter to Bell on July 24, 1949, Baker wrote: "Dr. Eckert, Dr. Mauchly, and Mr. Weiner have, several times, individually indicated a desire to discuss the instruction course with me. . . . Thursday they seemed very much upset. Friday they had several discussions among themselves, apparently considering what was to be done. . . . Yesterday, Dr. Mauchly wished again to discuss the matter with me at length. . . . He indicated that now that he knows what is wanted, all will go smoothly." But it was still touch and go, according to Baker, for later in the letter he said: "Mr. Joseph Chapline [the first lecturer] was given only a thirty second notice of the role he was to play. Mr. Auerbach. . . was apparently given an equal amount of time for preparation. . . . [Auerbach] had prepared notes at home, but had to start his lectures without them. In my opinion, Mr. Auerbach did an excellent job."

As the September 1 deadline moved closer, the news from Baker grew more ominous. His letter to Frank Bell on August 14, 1949, reported: "The BINAC completed only three hours of computation this week. The large number of troubles in the machine have prevented any extensive computation. The longest run was thirty minutes on a short repetitive diagnostic routine. . . . The high incidence of new troubles leaves [BINAC] in a less reliable condition now than [it was] at the beginning of the week."

Meeting the BINAC shipping date was not the only deadline Eckert and Mauchly were racing against. Because they wanted to make as much sales and publicity capital as could be generated by having an operational computer such as BINAC on the premises, three days of public demonstrations had been scheduled, from August 18 through the 20, for the press and potential customers. With BINAC in a condition little better than marginal, Mauchly bravely stood up before a crowd of reporters on the afternoon of

J. Presper Eckert (left, seated) and John Mauchly (right, seated) with key members of the BINAC team.

August 18 and calmly explained what they were about to see. The problem to be demonstrated was Poisson's equation for determining the deflection of an elastic plate, using a sixteen-by-sixteen grid. Mauchly told his listeners that the 196 values and the operating program virtually filled the machine's internal memory and that BINAC would compute the answer in eight minutes. Printing the answer, at the rate of seven characters per second, would take eight minutes more.

The BINAC demonstration, however, was really a ploy to guarantee a turnout. Mauchly intimated that the press had been called in for a "progress report" and at the present time his company had "nothing to sell." He then proceeded to direct everyone's attention to UNIVAC, a much more advanced machine to be unveiled in the near future. Much had been learned, said Mauchly, about electronic computing through the building of ENIAC and BINAC. To drive home this point, he told how both systems had helped to establish the feasibility of several new features to be incorporated in UNIVAC.

Eckert then took the floor. UNIVAC, he said, will be marketed primarily to the business user; its capabilities as a research calculator were not being exploited because of the limited demand for such machines. Launching into a simplified technical description of UNIVAC, Eckert cited the use of tape input/output and mercury delay-line memories, which considerably reduced the required vacuum tube complement. He said that UNIVAC would use an eight-channel metal tape instead of the plastic tape on BINAC. Eckert also emphasized the fact that no duplicate tape or memory elements would be needed in UNIVAC because of its unique automatic self-checking features.

At this point, guides who had been on the sidelines stood up and escorted the reporters downstairs to the BINAC test area. When they had occupied the designated vantage points around the machine, Joseph Weiner, equipped with a bullhorn to overcome the background noise, described the functions of each major component. After ten minutes, the reporters began drifting away to a makeshift bar that had been set up at one end of the room.

The whole show was repeated the next day for a horde of prospects, potential competitors, and curious onlookers. Guests representing Chrysler, Ford, General Motors, U.S. Steel, American Cyanimid, and more than twenty other companies were present. Gen. Leslie R. Groves, the highest ranking visitor from Remington Rand, was most intrigued by a display of metal tape to be used on future UNIVACs.

Eckert had revealed that it could be accelerated at a rate of thirty to forty "Gs" and be stopped within one-hundredth of a second without sustaining any damage. The tape could be moved past the write heads at the rate of ten feet per second and would record "twenty spots to the inch when manually recorded and one hundred spots to the inch when operated automatically." While Eckert was talking,

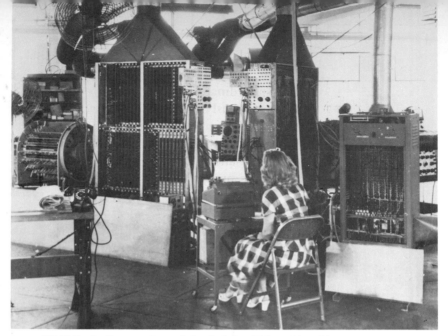

BINAC, *the first product of the fledgling Eckert-Mauchly company, was produced for Northrop Aviation Corporation in 1949. Large exhaust vents on top of the computer dissipate immense heat generated by the electronic tube circuits.*

The two main processors of BINAC and the electric typewriter (foreground) that served as its printer.

an ambitious young subordinate of Groves clipped off a piece of tape and surreptitiously slipped it into his pocket. Mauchly saw the theft and quietly walked over to him and asked for it. Groves, who was standing nearby, watched as the red-faced young man handed the tape to Mauchly. As they walked away, Groves nudged the culprit and, with a smile and a fatherly nod, said, "Nice try."

The next day a delegation of twenty government officials from the National Bureau of Standards and the Bureau of the Census arrived to witness a test run of BINAC. For this particular session, BINAC was required to operate faultlessly for a total of three hours in a six-hour time frame. The test problem was a routine involving random numbers and multiplication and division that had been run many times before in diagnostic checks. Once the acoustic delay-line memory had been loaded, the processing began and continued uninterrupted for fifty minutes until an arithmetic error terminated the run. The fault was corrected in three minutes, the processor was restarted, and the problem ran for twelve minutes before being stopped by the same error. Additional adjustments were made, and the machine ran without interruption for the rest of the session. The test was rated a success.

On August 28 a crew of twelve men elbowed their way around BINAC, checking the configurations of circuits against final layout prints and schematics. Preparations for shipment had already begun. Cables were labeled, wires stowed. That evening, composing his final letter to Frank Bell before returning to California, Baker wrote: "Tomorrow, the breakdown and crating process will begin. Crating is scheduled to continue through Tuesday and BINAC [will be airborne] Wednesday."

CHAPTER 12

Von Neumann's Project

When the director of the Institute for Advanced Study wrote to John von Neumann in June 1947 complaining about the need for more order and discipline in the computer project, the scholarly Frank Aydelotte was expressing his own personal concerns as well as trying to tidy things up for his successor, J. Robert Oppenheimer.

Oppenheimer, who was slated to take over the directorship a few months later, had been recruited by Lewis L. Strauss, a trustee of the institute and a member of the newly formed Atomic Energy Commission. The legislation creating the AEC was an act of government that would profoundly influence the individual careers of Oppenheimer and Strauss and also set the tone, for better and for worse, of their future relationship to each other.

Oppenheimer, a brilliant academic, had been the nucleus of a flourishing school of research in theoretical physics at the California Institute of Technology and the University of California throughout the 1930s. Later, with masterful skill, he directed the work of hundreds of scientists and technicians who designed and built the world's first atomic weapons in an isolated security-tight compound near Los Alamos, New Mexico. That goal could not have been achieved without Oppenheimer's unique persuasive abilities, which enabled him to convince many of the country's top physicists and their families to literally cut themselves off from the world and move into the desert enclave for the duration of the war.

For some, the isolation they endured was like living in a pressure cooker that was on the verge of blowing up. But Oppenheimer managed to keep the lid on. By exuding a compelling personal magnetism that was described by one exposed to it as a "kind of intellectual sex appeal," Oppenheimer assuaged his autocratic superior, Gen. Leslie R. Groves, and charmed the egos of the scientific prima donnas he had gathered around him.

Apart from a shared commitment to the advancement of atomic research, Strauss had little in common with Oppenheimer. While in high school, Strauss became intrigued with the new field of radioactivity and hoped to go to a university and become a physicist. Lack of money forced him to abandon any thoughts of continuing his education, and he went to work as a salesman in his father's wholesale shoe company in Richmond, Virginia. In March 1917, at the age of twenty-one, Strauss joined Herbert Hoover's Commission for Relief in Belgium. Shortly after America's entry into World War I, the future American president was called home to become head of the United States Food Administration. Strauss returned with him, and Hoover, after being favorably impressed by some economic studies Strauss had prepared, appointed Strauss his personal secretary.

From this new vantage point, the young Strauss was poised to move swiftly into the upper echelons of international business and politics. At age twenty-three Strauss was named one of four American delegates who parleyed with

German counterparts in Brussels in March 1919 to work out the final terms of the armistice ending World War I.

In April 1919 Mortimer Schiff, head of the powerful Wall Street banking house of Kuhn, Loeb & Company, was in Paris on a mission for the American Red Cross. He crossed paths with the young diplomat and was sufficiently struck by his poise and quick mind to offer Strauss a position in his firm. Strauss accepted, worked hard, and within eight years had risen through the ranks to the post of general partner. His upward mobility in the United States Navy was equally spectacular. He enrolled in the naval reserve as a lieutenant commander in 1929 but saw no active duty until February 1941, when he was ordered to become staff assistant to the navy's chief of ordnance. His innovative mind and organizational skills propelled him through a succession of increasingly important assignments until, at the war's end, he was a commodore, the equivalent of a brigadier general in the army. Two months before he left active service in January 1946, he was appointed rear admiral by President Harry S. Truman, becoming one of a few reservists ever to achieve flag rank.

Seven months after Strauss returned to Kuhn, Loeb, the McMahon Atomic Energy Act of 1946 was enacted by Congress. Among other things, the act established a new executive agency, the Atomic Energy Commission. Strauss was tapped to be one of the four commissioners serving under the chairman-designate, David E. Lilienthal. The law prescribed that every commissioner must divest himself of all stocks and other holdings, resign directorships on the boards of private corporations, and sever any affiliations with the securities business. While his position as a trustee of the Institute for Advanced Study was exempt, the partnership that Strauss held at Kuhn, Loeb was not. For Strauss, extricating himself from these bonds seemed an excruciating process and when faced with it, he said: "I feel like a man who is amputating his own leg."

If agreeing to accept the appointment to the commission

was painful for Strauss, it was a horrendous ordeal for David Lilienthal. During his previous distinguished service as chairman of the Tennessee Valley Authority, Lilienthal had incurred the wrath of Sen. Kenneth D. McKellar (Democrat of Tennessee) by refusing to turn the TVA into an agency of political patronage.

At the time of Lilienthal's nomination to the AEC, McKellar was a minority member of the Joint Congressional Committee on Atomic Energy, whose function it was to conduct hearings on the fitness of the chairman-designate. The Republican majority on the committee at first blocked McKellar's efforts to embarrass Lilienthal, but as the hearings wore on and sensing sympathy for McKellar's probings from their own constituents, they let him have his way. McKellar, in deprecating Lilienthal's liberal political views, implied that Lilienthal was soft on communism, a dangerous label for any public figure in the witch-hunting days of the late 1940s. (Lilienthal was eventually confirmed by the Senate.)

The long hearings virtually immobilized the top level of the Atomic Energy Commission, throwing much added work on that body's general advisory council. Oppenheimer, who had been appointed to the council by President Truman and named its chairman by his fellow members, bore the brunt of this overload. While Strauss and the other commissioners-designate sat in the first row of the hearing room during the eighty-five-day inquisition of Lilienthal, Oppenheimer, who believed his first responsibility was to his students in California, found himself spending more time on transcontinental flights or in Washington at the AEC than in the classroom. Considering his discomfort at having to mind the store in Washington and the fact that he felt out of step with the way the administration was moving on nuclear issues, Oppenheimer should not be faulted for wanting to put as much space as he could between himself and the imbroglio in Washington.

The divergence in viewpoints was not a new development but had been evident in one of Oppenheimer's first meetings with the president. Shortly after Japan surrendered, Truman had called Oppenheimer to the White House to ask his help in getting legislation through Congress that would prohibit sharing atomic secrets with the country's allies and help assure American dominance in this field. Truman summed up his position by declaring: "The first thing to do is define the national problem." Oppenheimer, obviously at odds with Truman's jingoistic posture on nuclear matters, replied, "Perhaps it would first be better to define the international problem." From this point on, Oppenheimer responded to the president's questions in such a desultory manner that Truman broke off the conversation to ask if there was anything wrong. Oppenheimer replied: "I feel we have blood on our hands." Truman countered: "Never mind. It'll all come out in the wash."

When Strauss become aware of Oppenheimer's distaste for the frequent treks back and forth across the country, he hit upon a plan that would eliminate the need for the transcontinental shuttling. Other trustees at the Institute for Advanced Study had empowered Strauss to find a successor for Dr. Frank Aydelotte, who had announced his intention to retire in the fall of 1947. Strauss approached several members of the institute's faculty, including von Neumann and the venerable Albert Einstein, to ascertain their opinions of Oppenheimer. The consensus was positive, although Einstein would offer no comment about Oppenheimer, nor would he suggest a candidate of his own. But in response to a question by Strauss asking what qualities the trustees should look for in selecting a director of the institute, Einstein replied: "Ah, that I can do easily. . . . You should look for a very quiet man who will not disturb people who are thinking."

On a trip to the West Coast early in 1947, Strauss drew Oppenheimer aside and broached the matter of the directorship to him. Strauss was taken aback by Oppenheimer's failure to warm quickly to the proposal, but he had not known about Oppenheimer's first brush with the institute twelve years earlier. During a holiday visit to his parents in New York, Oppenheimer had been invited to Princeton by Prof. Herman Weyl, one of the first distinguished members of the institute's mathematics faculty. Weyl had been deputized to persuade Oppenheimer to accept an invitation to join the institute. In a letter to his brother Frank on January 11, 1935, Oppenheimer described that visit: "Princeton is a madhouse; its solipsistic luminaries shining in separate and helpless desolation. Einstein is completely cuckoo.... I could be of no use at such a place, but it took a lot of conversation and arm waving to get Weyl to take a *no*."

Strauss, however, was persistent. He and Oppenheimer had several conversations during the ensuing weeks, and, finally, in April 1947, the trustees announced that Oppenheimer would succeed Aydelotte the following October.

If von Neumann had been concerned about the stance the new director would take on the computer project, he need not have been. Oppenheimer turned out to be an enthusiastic supporter who presided over the completion of a new building for von Neumann's team, supplanting the temporary quarters arranged by Aydelotte. Its location—about a quarter of a mile away from the others in the complex— seemed to be a concession to Aydelotte's desire to keep the computer workers geographically isolated from the institute's academic mainstream.

Von Neumann's lofty position in the scientific world enabled him to attract a stellar group of mathematicians and engineers. In addition to Herman H. Goldstine, there were several other outstanding talents who came to Princeton in early 1946. One was Julian Bigelow who had worked during the war on automatic computing and control projects with Norbert Wiener at the Massachusetts Institute of Technology. Bigelow, who had been glowingly endorsed by Wiener, had also done important work for the Fire Control

Division and Applied Mathematics Panel of the National Defense Research Committee. Another NRDC alumnus was Ralph J. Slutz, a physicist, who was considered an expert in electronics.

Government and the halls of academia, however, were by no means the only source of expertise for the computer project. The private sector contributed its share, too— James H. Pomerene and Willis H. Ware from Hazeltine Electronics. Finally, there was Arthur Burks, whose association with the project, while brief, was nonetheless fruitful because of his ability to apply his unique grasp of the interrelationships subtly linking mathematics, philosophy, and engineering in the overall design of the system.

The paths followed by von Neumann and the Eckert-Mauchly Computer Corporation in their pursuit of a common goal seemed poles apart. Eckert and Mauchly, grappling with one business crisis after another, were constantly goaded by the need to push ahead rapidly, to get things done. The design and construction of the first UNIVAC, therefore, was a continuous struggle against clock and calendar. Working conditions in the tranquil environment of the Institute for Advanced Study, however, were quite different.

Leon Harmon, a member of von Neumann's team at Princeton, recalled in 1972: "The atmosphere was one of great camaraderie. There were, I suppose, at most about twenty people involved. . . . Everyone interacted rather closely. The pace was leisurely." But not for long. According to Harmon, there were two kinds of pressures building up. The first involved the control unit: "Bigelow was taking a rather long time with it . . . because it was indeed an exceedingly complicated thing to design and put down on paper and because [Bigelow was] a perfectionist. He insisted on having things exactly right. The second pressure built up later as users [of the computer] became more and more numerous." The steadily growing roster of projects and problems waiting to be run on the computer pushed the final completion date farther into the future, and the expanding user base stimulated demand for more capacity, which required the engineering group to continue its work long after the initial start-up.

Nearly six years elapsed between the time von Neumann assembled his team in Princeton in 1946 and the official completion date of the computer in January 1952. Harmon cites two reasons for the lengthy gestation: "The atmosphere [at the institute] was academic in the true sense of the word, rather than commercial [which generates] more realistic and hard-nosed attitudes towards schedules and deadlines. But I think the main reason [was] Julian Bigelow's lust for precision, for elegance, for completeness, for perfection, and for a certain amount of esthetics." Bigelow's approach to chassis design, for example, required "an enormous amount of planning and cutting and trying and polishing." Rejecting the electronic assembly practices then in vogue, which called for mounting tubes and components on flat metal sheets and sliding them into racks like shelves in a bookcase, Bigelow opted for a highly unorthodox three-dimensional configuration. Because parts were installed on a curved chassis, wiring was not limited to the conventional X-Y axis of a planar surface. While this arrangement multiplied options, threading a wire from one point to another, ordinarily routine, became a matter of critical delicacy. As a result, Bigelow's design was as much a work of art as it was an engineering masterpiece.

Reaching faulty components in the three-dimensional architecture was also difficult. Elements in the lower part of the machine were "nested," and although they were fashioned to operate with a high degree of reliability, outages did occur. For Harmon, even the removal of a defective tube was no small matter: "The machine was built like a chimney. The tubes were all in the lining of the chimney and you stood outside. So to get at any tube, you had to reach in and around and because of chassis interconnections [some wiring had to be unsoldered]. Also [to reach] such things as the pulse generators [which were shielded], additional demounting [was required]. And while removing a Williams cathode ray tube was not too difficult, one had to take out the amplifier first."

Getting the computer ready to run a problem was a formidable task and required considerable expertise. But unfamiliarity with the machine's basic design and structure did not necessarily disqualify anyone from operating it. Yet, there was some hand holding. Harmon recalled that the computer "was sufficiently delicate with respect to watching for various of the electrical parameters, that either an engineer or a [skilled] operator had to be on hand to make sure the thing wasn't blown up." Current for the tube filaments had to be turned up gradually because a sudden jolt would burn them out. Plate voltages were raised slowly through progressively higher stages until the desired power level was reached. "The entire set of operations ... was a cookbook formulation intricate in the sense [that] a number of steps had to be taken in the right kind of sequence."

When the tedious business of flipping switches, turning rheostats, and monitoring dancing needles on panel instruments was done, the computer, from the perspective of mathematicians privileged to use it, took on a near magical quality. For decades intriguing theories remained unproved and critical problems unsolved because no one could cope with the sheer magnitude of computations to be dealt with before the prize could be seized. Now all this had changed. A seemingly impenetrable barrier had been breached, and treasures beyond measure lay ripe for the plucking.

Mark Twain is reported to have said that everybody talks about the weather but nobody ever does anything about it. Now someone could. In 1946 von Neumann and his associates had conducted some preliminary numerical studies of weather patterns on the ENIAC. The findings coming out

J. Robert Oppenheimer (left) and John von Neumann with von Neumann's computer at the Institute for Advanced Study, Princeton, New Jersey.

of those experiments were encouraging enough to warrant further exploration. As a result, an investigation of fundamental problems in dynamic meteorology was one of the first scientific projects scheduled for the institute's computer. Dr. Jule G. Charney, a renowned meteorologist, was brought in to direct this effort. Charney's strategy was to attack the problems in stages. He developed a sequence of idealized mathematical models of the atmosphere in which each successive model was slightly more complex than its predecessor. Charney's first opportunity to test these models on a computer came in 1950 when the Ballistic Research Laboratory permitted him to use the ENIAC in Aberdeen. Later, more advanced models were run on the institute's computer after it was completed in January 1952.

A pinnacle in Charney's research was reached in early

1953 when he and his associates produced a meteorological model that successfully pinpointed the origin of storms. Until then, these violent atmospheric disturbances had defied prediction, confounded experts, and seriously flawed efforts to gain greater recognition for the practice of weather forecasting. A crucial experiment that confirmed the validity of the model was a simulation of a severe storm that had struck the Appalachian region on November 25, 1950. Thousands of readings gathered from observatories throughout the United States in the weeks before that event were processed by the institute's computer. Under the guidance of the model, data were churned out charting the course of the storm and correctly identifying the geographic areas sustaining the most damage. Further corroboration of the model's accuracy was provided by similar after-the-fact simulations of two other major storms that struck the eastern United States on November 12, 1952, and November 5, 1953.

Aydelotte's policy of keeping the computer project insulated from the mainstream of the institute's intellectual pursuits continued under Oppenheimer, but not because the new director nurtured strong feelings on the matter. It would have been rather difficult to do otherwise. The location of the computer building a quarter of a mile from others in the complex and the fact that most of the academic explorations of the institute proper had little in common with what von Neumann was doing there kept communication between the two groups to a minimum.

There was one occasion during the year, however, when everyone affiliated with the institute got together. The annual spring dance was a social event that enabled the computer project's electricians and wiremen to rub elbows with the most learned men in America. Oppenheimer presided graciously over these functions, trying at all times to put everyone at ease. He could be just as enthusiastic and solicitous introducing such a world-renowned visitor as

Niels Bohr, the Danish physicist, to a machinist as he would for the most distinguished member of the institute's faculty.

If the members and staff of the institute had little in common in a professional way with the engineers on the computer project, there were opportunities, nevertheless, for secretarial employees of both groups to intermingle. One day at noon, Libby Wooden, a computer project secretary, was on her way to meet a friend, a mathematics department clerical worker, at the institute cafeteria. When she started to cross the field adjacent to the main building, she spotted a head of flowing white hair disappearing and reappearing moments later from behind a hedge in the distance. Moving closer, she discovered the venerable Albert Einstein, who, for some inexplicable reason, was picking things out of the dirt along the path. Puzzled, she hurried to the cafeteria to tell her friend about his strange behavior. The friend, who had witnessed similar incidents at other times, cleared up the mystery. Because of Einstein's failing health, his doctor had forbidden him to smoke. The ban was thought easy to enforce because Einstein never carried any money and any personal needs, such as tobacco, were supplied by his daughter or his housekeeper. However, no one had accounted for Einstein's resourcefulness. Whenever he wanted to indulge, he would scrounge discarded cigarette butts along the path, empty the tobacco into his pipe, and steal off to some remote spot on the grounds to enjoy it.

While a by-product of establishing von Neumann's computer project at the institute was an increase in Einstein's tobacco supply, this was not the only benefit the old gentleman derived from its presence. One morning, Herman Goldstine told Leon Harmon that Einstein's daughter and housekeeper intended to give him a record turntable for his approaching birthday and they needed some advice. Harmon agreed to help, and because it was to be a surprise, he went over to see them when Einstein was not at home. The record player would be an ideal addition, the ladies told

Harmon, to the tuner-amplifier-speaker system that the members of the institute had given to Einstein the year before. Could Harmon find a good one, they asked, for about $25.00? Taken aback by their unfamiliarity with the cost of high-fidelity components, Harmon replied that the price would be four times that amount, possibly more. Oh, they said, they could not afford that much and thanked him for his trouble.

Harmon left, dismayed that this great man, in his final years, would be denied the pleasure of listening to classical music on long-playing records. On an impulse, Harmon went to Oppenheimer's office with a proposition. Raise money for the record player by soliciting contributions from institute members, he pleaded, and he would see that it was installed properly. Oppenheimer readily agreed, offering to make up the balance if the collection fell short of its goal.

After several visits by Harmon to Einstein's home to install wiring and get everything ready so that the player could be plugged right in when presented to him, Oppenheimer and Harmon arrived at Einstein's doorstep on the appointed day carrying a large box wrapped with metal foil and garnished with ribbons and bows. They were ushered into a study where Einstein was enjoying a quiet birthday celebration with a few guests. After introductions and some chitchat, Oppenheimer said: "Professor, we brought you a present. We can't stay too long and perhaps we could give it to you now."

Einstein took the box, clucking with pleasure at the beautiful wrapping. Running his hands over it for what seemed like minutes, Einstein went on to marvel at the technology that could produce such an attractive paper at a cost low enough to justify its use in this way. Finally Oppenheimer interrupted: "But Professor, there's something inside, too, that you should see." Oppenheimer then reached into his pocket and offered a pocketknife to snip the ribbon while

Harmon retrieved a pair of cutters from his toolbox for the same purpose. Einstein refused both, saying: "Oh, no, no, that's much too brutal." Instead, he slowly untied the knots, meticulously smoothing the ribbon before laying it over the back of a chair. Then he stopped to admire the wrapping again.

After another reminder by Oppenheimer that there was something inside, Einstein opened the box and clasped his hands in delight. Harmon removed the player and, after making the appropriate connections, gave a brief lecture and demonstration on the proper way to operate it. Einstein watched transfixed. Then the elder statesman of science, one of the few throughout history who have taught us more about the universe than all of their most learned peers, gave Harmon the thrill of his life. Grasping both of Harmon's hands in his, Einstein said: "You know, Mr. Harmon, you are a very good teacher."

CHAPTER 13

Into the Big Time

The sky was black and rain beat on the window as Miss Mary Campbell peered into the darkness early one evening in October 1949. Suddenly a flash of light illuminated a ridge in the distance, and moments later she heard a rumbling that sounded like thunder. Members of several other households in the vicinity of Port Deposit, Maryland, had also seen the flash and heard the noise. And some, for a quarter of an hour or so earlier, had noticed the whirring of a plane's engines in the clouds overhead.

An alarm sounded in the firehouse of the Perryville Volunteers, and twenty minutes later fire fighters were converging on the burning remnants of a twin-engined Beechcraft, which, before coming to rest on a wooded hillside, had cut a swath almost 500 feet long through the treetops. At the time of the crash, the Beechcraft, a private plane owned by the American Totalisator Company, was flying Henry L. Straus home from a business appointment in New York. Straus, Arthur J. Johnson, another passenger who was also general manager of AmTote, and the pilot and copilot were killed instantly.

The death of Straus left a gaping void between the struggling young computer builders and their primary source of funding, the American Totalisator Company. In all dealings with AmTote, Straus had been their mentor and spokesman. At the time Straus presented his Eckert-Mauchly bailout plan to AmTote's board of directors, Charles A. and Gurnee Munn had viewed the proposal with reservations but finally agreed to support it. But with Straus gone and no one available with comparable talents to replace him, the Munn brothers moved quickly to extricate themselves from the problems in Philadelphia.

On November 1, 1949, six days after the AmTote plane crashed, Gurnee Munn resigned from the computer company's board of directors. Oscar C. Levy, who had been selected by the Munns to be the new chairman and preside over the severing of AmTote's ties to the Eckert-Mauchly Computer Corporation, wasted no time in getting down to business.

Immediately after his installation as chairman at a board meeting on November 4, 1949, Levy called for progress reports on the search for a new financial backer. Eckert, who had visited the offices of Remington Rand in New York City a few days earlier, reported that the business machine maker had expressed "a definite interest in our enterprise." George Eltgroth added that contacts had also been made with Bendix Aviation, International Telephone & Telegraph, and Hazeltine Electronics. T. Wistar Brown reported that the Nielsen Corporation had contacted some private investors in the Chicago area who were considered excellent prospects. Mauchly, who had been delegated to scout the financial community for a firm to represent them in future negotiations, announced that Drexel & Company had been retained to act as investigator and intermediary.

At a meeting of the board on November 22, 1949, Levy revealed that he had approached Donald H. Sherwood, a director of the Mergenthaler Linotype Corporation, about the Eckert-Mauchly opportunity. Levy said that he had offered all of AmTote's Eckert-Mauchly stock at prices similar to those originally paid by AmTote but that any response would be delayed until Mergenthaler's director of research could study the situation. Eltgroth reported that Hazeltine had broken off the talks, but that there were other nibbles by Westinghouse Electric, Federal Telephone, and Hughes Aircraft. IBM's Thomas Watson, Jr., had received the Eckert-Mauchly emissaries but backed off when his legal counsel expressed concern over antitrust complications if America's largest business machine supplier took control of the only company then engaged in electronic computer development. Eckert and T. Wistar Brown had also won an audience with Remington Rand president James H. Rand, who, while making no direct overtures, gave the impression that he wanted to talk some more.

Rand, a canny bargainer, would not make a move until he had the upper hand. Time was on his side and he could afford to wait—but Eckert and Mauchly could not. Oscar Levy was getting increasing pressure from the Munns to find a buyer, and when he convened a meeting of the board on December 29, 1949, the situation was anything but promising. Because of its diffident response to his overtures, George Eltgroth said that ITT should be crossed off the list. He had more discouraging news: The negotiators for Hughes Aircraft Company would not continue discussions unless they could be assured that key Eckert-Mauchly personnel would agree to move to California and that there would be no costly lease-cancellation charge imposed by the transfer of operations from Philadelphia to the West Coast. Next, Levy revealed that the talks with Burroughs

Adding Machine Company and Mergenthaler Linotype had hit some snags and were temporarily stalled. T. Wistar Brown tried to sound an upbeat note: Although no date had been agreed upon for another meeting with Remington Rand, that company was still an "excellent prospect."

John Mauchly then reviewed efforts recently made to secure an $800,000 loan from the Reconstruction Finance Corporation. He said that Dr. S. N. Alexander of the National Bureau of Standards and J. G. McPherson of the Bureau of the Census were pulling what strings they could to hurry the company's application through the various departments of that agency. The loan, if approved, would come none too soon. A critical cash crunch was crippling relations with suppliers. This point was addressed in a memo written by the head of the purchasing department, which Calvin Bosin, the company's treasurer, read to the board members. It concluded on a disturbing note: "If some payments are not met in the near future, we will reach a point where we will be unable to obtain materials necessary for continued production on the UNIVAC. At the present time, the situation. . . is both embarrassing and difficult in some cases to obtain deliveries."

At the next meeting of the board on January 12, 1950, T. Wistar Brown recounted the highlights of a discussion a few days earlier with Arthur Draper of Remington Rand. Draper had put forth no specific proposals but wanted "to work out a plan satisfactory to all concerned." Eckert and Mauchly, who were also present at the meeting with Draper, had emphasized that any agreement that might be reached should ensure that while Remington Rand would own a majority stock interest in their company, the Eckert-Mauchly Computer Corporation "would continue as a corporate entity with protection to assure the accumulation of assets and to prevent their transfer or diversion." Eltgroth then attempted to satisfy a part of this requirement by suggesting a royalty plan that while not actually preventing any attempt to transfer assets would nevertheless protect the Eckert-Mauchly interests. The meeting with Draper ended after Eltgroth had gone over several installment procedures whereby controlling stock could be transferred to Remington Rand in return for royalties on sales of equipment covered by Eckert-Mauchly patents.

Levy, fearing that a live prospect that was nearly hooked might slip away, hastily interjected that American Totalisator was willing and ready to negotiate with anyone who would bargain in good faith for its Eckert-Mauchly stock interests and that AmTote would "give proper consideration to the interests of all concerned."

By the end of January 1950, James H. Rand, who was monitoring the situation by telephone and telegraph from the fantail of his yacht *Tara*, which lay moored to a dock in Palm Beach, Florida, sensed that the time had come to make his move. He instructed J. A. W. Simpson, a Remington Rand corporate attorney, to dispatch an offering letter to American Totalisator. Simpson, who was well aware of the Munns' plight, knew how to turn the screws: "After a very careful and thorough examination of Eckert-Mauchly and its prospects, and a review of its 1949 financial statements, we feel that it must be apparent to you, as it is to us, that without additional substantial cash advances of more than $1,000,000, Eckert-Mauchly cannot hope to complete the development of a marketable electronic computer ... and that in their present financial condition ... and the present situation in the development of their electronic computer, you cannot hope to recover out of its assets anything more than a nominal portion of your loans to that corporation, and that you would realize nothing on your investments in its stock were you to proceed now with any legal steps for collection of any part of the company's indebtedness to you."

Having effectively neutralized any bargaining advantage American Totalisator might have had, Simpson offered to purchase all of its Eckert-Mauchly shares as well as settle the computer company's indebtedness to AmTote for the sum of $375,365. One month later, Simpson wrote to Rand: "I have the pleasure to advise you that yesterday, March 1st, we purchased from the American Totalisator Company, 12,-400 shares of common stock and 2,857 shares of preferred stock issued to [AmTote] by the Eckert-Mauchly Computer Corporation.... We now own all of the issued and outstanding shares ... except 1,500 shares of common stock and 1,500 shares of preferred stock which stand in the name of 13 individuals.... I have also in my possession the resignations of Ector O. Munn, O. C. Levy, C. A. Munn and H. C. Robinson, as directors of the Eckert-Mauchly Computer Corporation.... The Totalisator Company delivered a full and complete release of any and all claims against [Eckert-Mauchly]... in other words, a complete separation and termination."

Rand settled back in his chair on his yacht, savoring his triumph. He had come a long way since that day in 1915 when he had resigned from his father's company because the elder Rand had refused to expand and diversify his small but profitable bank ledger manufacturing business. James Rand, Jr., then borrowed $10,000 to produce and market an invention of his, a visible index "Kardex" filing system. It was the first step in assembling, under a single corporate structure, what the young Rand envisioned as a broad line of office products.

A year later he paid off the loan and borrowed another $50,000 from the Chase National Bank. In 1925, in response to his mother's plea—"Why don't you two boys stop fighting?"—he and his father joined forces and formed the Rand Kardex Corporation. In a stroke of supersalesmanship, the younger Rand then persuaded a group of bankers to lend him $25 million to build the "greatest office supply company the world has ever seen." Rand engineered this feat by promising to pay back the bank loan by issuing bonds secured by the assets of the companies he bought. A daring plan, fraught with risks, but it worked. By 1927 Rand had acquired the Library Bureau of Boston, builder of quality library and office furniture, the Safe-Cabinet Company, the Dalton Adding Machine Company, and the Powers Tabulating Machine Company. And to cap this coup, he negotiated the purchase of the Remington Typewriter Company, creating a new corporate giant to be known as Remington Rand, Inc., until it merged in 1955 with the Sperry Corporation.

Remington Rand's first move into the world of advanced technology did not occur until 1946. At that time the nucleus of a new research laboratory was established at South Norwalk, Connecticut, and was initially staffed by a few engineers who had worked on some electronic gear that Remington Rand supplied to a government guided-missile project during the war. During the next two years, this small group was gradually fleshed out with new hirings and transfers from other operating divisions of the company. By 1948 the laboratory had grown sufficiently in stature to enable James Rand to persuade Gen. Leslie R. Groves to head it. Groves, whose reputation as a top-notch administrator prompted Rand to recruit him, presided over a program modernizing the old mechanical Powers tabulating machine, a standard Remington Rand product for more than two decades.

Groves also was a member of the Remington Rand management team that engineered the acquisition of Eckert-Mauchly. About a year after that takeover, the press was again invited to Philadelphia to witness the formal acceptance of UNIVAC Model-One-Number-One by the Bureau of the Census. Dr. Edward U. Condon, director of the

National Bureau of Standards, the agency charged with overseeing the development and purchase of all computers sold to the federal government, noted that the bureau "has responsibility for seven computers intended for the Air Force, Army, Navy, Bureau of the Census and other federal agencies."

Five of the seven were UNIVACs. The other two, SEAC (*Standards Eastern Automatic Computer*) and SWAC (*Standards Western Automatic Computer*), were built by the National Bureau of Standards itself. Planned as a stop-gap to provide computational capability until a UNIVAC was completed, SEAC and SWAC were limited internal development projects meant to fade away once more advanced and reliable machines came onto the scene. But when the promised delivery date for the first UNIVAC was pushed further into the future, which in 1949 meant a two-year wait, both SEAC and SWAC were upgraded to major projects. Until the delivery of the first UNIVAC to the Census Bureau in 1951, SEAC, completed in June 1950, was considered the fastest general-purpose, automatically sequenced electronic computer in operation. SWAC, its sister machine, which was undergoing evaluation tests in the National Bureau of Standards mathematical laboratories in Los Angeles in June 1951, was pressed into service later that year.

Surveying the faces of the Remington Rand directors as he sat at the head of the table in a private room of the University Club in New York one morning in November 1951, James Rand had good reason to be in good humor. He headed a company that, a few months earlier, had taken a giant step forward in the eyes of the business community by delivering the world's first commercial computer to the Census Bureau. And this was only the beginning: His Eckert-Mauchly subsidiary had already won orders for eight additional systems. Now, at this meeting of his board, he

Lieut. Gen. Leslie R. Groves, with John W. Mauchly (left) and J. Presper Eckert, Jr., inspects the first model of UNIVAC during its construction in Philadelphia.

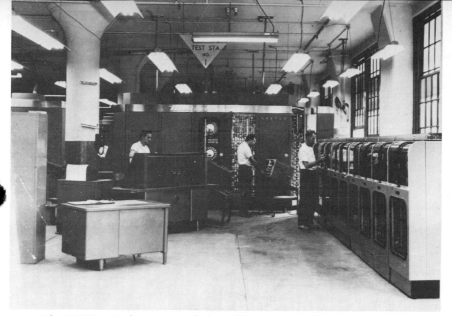

The UNIVAC I during tests before delivery to the U.S. Bureau of the Census.

J. Presper Eckert, Jr., at the control console of UNIVAC before its official acceptance by the U.S. Bureau of the Census in 1951. Others in the photo are (left to right): James Rand, president of Remington Rand; Dr. Roy V. Peel, director of the Census Bureau; Lieut. Gen. Leslie R. Groves, former head of the Manhattan Project; Charles Sawyer, Secretary of Commerce; and Dr. Edward Condon, director of the National Bureau of Standards.

was about to secure approval for another coup—the purchase of Engineering Research Associates of St. Paul, Minnesota.

ERA, under the leadership of John Parker, had grown fast but was seriously short of working capital. Rand, as he had earlier in Philadelphia, moved in and provided the cash to keep ERA going. In two swift strokes he had firmly consolidated Remington Rand's unchallenged position as the world's major supplier of electronic computers.

CHAPTER 14

UNIVAC Becomes a Household Word

The red light on the television camera flicked on. Charles Collingwood, seated in a CBS studio in New York City, smiled confidently at his unseen audience across America as he revealed the network's plans for broadcast coverage of the 1952 presidential election: "Here at CBS we are making elaborate preparations to bring you the results of the night of November 4th, just as quickly and as accurately as is humanly possible. Matter of fact, we want to bring them to you faster and more accurately than is humanly possible, so we have enlisted the aid of Remington Rand's UNIVAC.... If UNIVAC behaves the way we think it will, we'll all know the winner long before the final votes are counted."

During the weeks preceding Collingwood's announcement, political analysts, statisticians, and computer programmers had huddled in meetings in Philadelphia conjuring up ways to endow UNIVAC with sufficient expertise to predict the winner of the Eisenhower-Stevenson race after only a small portion of the votes had been tallied. Months earlier, when UNIVAC was first brought to the attention of CBS, the experts at Remington Rand had blithely assumed that programming the system for analyzing voting patterns across America would be a routine undertaking. However, as the weeks rolled by and the election night deadline loomed ever closer, the experts thought that they had bitten off more than they could chew.

It had started as a simple business barter arrangement. In

Charles Collingwood, CBS newscaster, at a UNIVAC supervisory control desk, used as a prop in the CBS studios in New York City on election night, November 4, 1952.

April 1952 a representative of the network had come to Remington Rand with a proposition. The office equipment manufacturer would be given nationwide television exposure at no cost in return for the temporary use of a hundred or so typewriters and adding machines. The quid pro quo was to be part of the programming: As television cameras panned around the huge studio (which would be filled with workers diligently tapping the keys of adding machines and typewriters), a camera would zoom in over someone's shoulder from time to time to focus briefly on the Remington Rand logotype emblazoned above the keyboard. The deal was sealed with a handshake, but before the CBS man reached the door, a suggestion by a Remington Rand publicist stopped him in his tracks.

Sustaining viewer interest during the tedious hours of reporting the vote, precinct by precinct and state by state, was a tough challenge for broadcasters. Break the monotony, said the publicist, by predicting the winner with an electronic computer and viewers will stay with you all night to see if the computer is right or wrong. This extra bit of show biz, which might possibly add some life to a slow-moving story, was enthusiastically endorsed by CBS management, but professional newscasters did not know whether to take the matter seriously or not. Their general uneasiness was evident in a response by Walter Cronkite (then chief Washington correspondent for CBS) to a question by Dorothy Fuldheim during an evening news broadcast by WEWS-TV in Cleveland, Ohio:

> DOROTHY FULDHEIM: Tell me, Walter, what are you going to do to report this very historic election?
>
> WALTER CRONKITE: Well, this year we've got the same basic formula that we had before, which is, of course, straight reporting of how the returns are coming in. However, we do have a little gimmickry this year which I think is most interesting, and may turn out to be some-

thing more than gimmickry. We're using an electronic brain which a division of Remington Rand has in Philadelphia.

DOROTHY FULDHEIM: What does it do?

WALTER CRONKITE: It's going to predict the outcome of the election, hour by hour, based on returns at the same time periods on the election nights in 1944 and 1948. Scientists, whom we used to call long hairs, have been working on correlating the facts [for these predictions] for the past two or three months. . . . Actually, we're not depending too much on this machine. It may be just a sideshow . . . and then again it may turn out to be of great value to some people.

At the time Cronkite was telling Dorothy Fuldheim that UNIVAC might be of great value, the long hairs in Philadelphia were fearful that its widely publicized debut on television would be a flop. Before UNIVAC could be programmed to rapidly analyze the election night returns, mathematical equations had to be formulated describing trends and voting patterns for thousands of political subdivisions throughout the United States. This massive undertaking was rendered more difficult by the fact that there was virtually no precedent for an analysis of this magnitude. The statisticians, laboring over reams of data covering the two previous presidential elections, had no existing body of expertise to guide them.

Finally, a workable method for processing the data gradually took shape. Now the experts could direct their attention to the practical business of getting ready to run the problem when the returns started coming in. Because the only available UNIVAC systems were in Remington Rand's factory in Philadelphia, a special Teletype line was reserved for transmitting the vote counts from CBS election night headquarters in New York. Three UNIVAC systems figured in the plan: One to actually process the data and be

Walter Cronkite, veteran CBS anchorman, is briefed on UNIVAC's fine points by console operator Harold Sweeney during preparations for election night, 1952, while J. Presper Eckert, Jr. looks on.

seen on television; a second UNIVAC, behind the scenes to carefully check the output of the first; and a third, on standby, in the event of an emergency.

By 6:00 P.M. election night, all was in readiness. The New York–Philadelphia Teletype circuit had been checked and rechecked. The primary UNIVAC and its backup systems were in excellent operating condition, and the scientists in the Remington Rand computer center in Philadelphia were busily fine tuning procedures in a series of dry runs.

When the first returns were flashed from CBS in New York, each set was printed in triplicate. The copies were then handed to the operators of three Unitypers who rapidly converted the alphanumeric information to magnetized bits on magnetic tape. When a batch of returns had been run through the Unitypers, their tapes were mounted on three Uniservo drives of the second UNIVAC and a comparison run was made to detect inconsistencies. If a precinct count on one tape differed from the comparable entries on the other two, the discrepancy was immediately called out on a printer. Then the latest total for that precinct was located on the original Teletype and the correct count reentered into the system, which produced a validated listing on a fourth reel of magnetic tape.

While the most recent tallies were being transcribed on the fourth tape, all of the precinct totals were sorted into a predetermined sequence. At the same time, the data were subjected to three additional tests. First, the number of districts reporting was checked against the total number of districts in the area under study. Second, the reported vote on any given pass had to be at least as high as the previously reported total. And finally, the major party votes in each district were compared with similar data compiled for that constituency in 1944 and 1948.

The vote totals were then in the proper format for entry into the primary UNIVAC system. For this phase, composite analyses of returns in the 1944 and 1948 elections had been stored in the computer's memory in addition to a comprehensive history of state-by-state voting trends dating back to 1928. From this information district profiles were charted that defined the relative strengths of the major party registrations and the so-called independent vote.

The district totals fed into UNIVAC's processor from the fourth tape were compared to the historical records of those districts in the computer's memory. Then a final vote probability was determined for each locality. These voting patterns became the basis for a general preliminary estimate of the total national vote for each candidate. Adjustments were then factored in at prescribed intervals to correct any discrepancies that arose between the actual vote counted for a district and the voting pattern selected for that district. In this way, as the evening wore on and larger percentages of the total vote cast could be fed into the system, each subsequent projection could be based more on hard facts and less on assumptions.

Election night, 1952. As early returns filter in, operators type data on these machines, which are connected to magnetic-tape units in the background. Tapes are then placed on UNIVAC, which compares the initial counts with voting patterns in previous elections and then issues predictions.

By 9:00 P.M., with early returns streaming in from the eastern and central time zones, the huge CBS election night headquarters in New York City was buzzing with activity. Telephones jangled. Teletype machines clacked noisily. Scribbled figures on scraps of paper were passed hastily to toteboard operators. Then the director in the control room, scanning an array of monitors, barked an order. Instantly the face of Charles Collingwood flashed on screens in living rooms across the nation as the comforting voice of Walter Cronkite told viewers what was going on.

WALTER CRONKITE: And now to find out what perhaps this all means, at least in the electronic age, let's turn to that electronic brain, UNIVAC, with a report from Charles Collingwood.

COLLINGWOOD: UNIVAC, our fabulous mathematical brain, is down in Philadelphia mulling over the returns that we've sent it so far. A few minutes ago, I asked him what his prediction was, and he sent me back a very caustic answer. He said that if we continue to be so late in sending him results, it's going to take him a few minutes to find out just what the prediction is going to be. So he's not ready yet with the predictions but we're going to go to him in just a little while.

As Collingwood was telling his audience that UNIVAC was not ready for a prediction, it had, in fact, already made one. The business about needing more time was a cover-up. Unknown to Collingwood, the folks in Philadelphia had fabricated that story to save face.

A few minutes earlier, with only three million votes counted, an astounding forecast rolled off the electric typewriter that functioned as the computer's printer. UNIVAC gave 43 states and 438 electoral votes to Dwight D. Eisenhower. Adlai E. Stevenson would capture only 5 states and 93 electoral votes. The odds for victory by the Republican candidate were predicted by UNIVAC as 100 to one or better in his favor—an Eisenhower landslide.

Computer programmers huddled around the printer in shocked silence. Throughout the campaign, pollsters and political analysts had been predicting a close election that would not be decided until the wee hours of the next morning. Yet with only 7 percent of the vote counted, UNIVAC had gone way out on a limb. Too far, it seemed to those watching the state-by-state breakdown emerge from the printer. What was this? Several southern states going Republican? That hadn't happened in seventy-two years! Something was wrong.

A murmur in the crowd: There must be a glitch in the program. Then a mad scramble. Everyone, grabbing code books and programming records, frantically flicked through reams of data, hoping, by some miracle, that any error that had escaped notice would now surface and be recognized. But after several minutes of fruitless page turning, punctuated by answering telephoned appeals from New York to get UNIVAC's act together, the search was called off.

Arthur F. Draper, Remington Rand's director of advanced research and the man in charge of election night operations in Philadelphia, agreed with his advisers that something drastic had to be done to bring UNIVAC back to its senses. They decided to go right to the heart of the matter and arbitrarily change the factor—so carefully fine tuned through months of preparation—that extrapolated the number of returns actually received into estimated final totals for each state.

Fortunately, this was a simple procedure. One merely had to run the program to the breakpoint where the critical factor was computed, stop the run, type in a new figure from the supervisory control desk, and resume processing. Within two minutes, a new set of totals began rolling off the printer. A chastened UNIVAC reported 28 states and 317 electoral votes for Eisenhower. Much better, but not good enough for the thoroughly shaken crew in Philadelphia.

Still hedging, they tweaked the formula again. This time UNIVAC called the election a toss-up. It gave twenty-four states to each candidate with Eisenhower leading in electoral votes by a scanty margin of 270 to 261. Breathing easier, and wiping perspiration from foreheads, the computer people in Philadelphia released these figures to CBS, which broadcast them on the network at 10:00 P.M.

By 11:00 P.M., however, Eisenhower votes were rolling in like a tidal wave, and UNIVAC, shrugging off the dampening influence of the twice-revised formula, swung back again to the original prediction of 100 to one odds in favor of the general. At midnight, in his recap of the evening's coverage, Collingwood asked Draper what went wrong:

COLLINGWOOD: An hour or so ago, UNIVAC suffered a momentary aberration. He gave us the odds on Eisenhower as only eight to seven . . . but came up later with the prediction that the odds were beyond counting, above 100 to one, in favor of Eisenhower's election. Let's go down to Philadelphia and see whether we can get an explanation of what happened from Mr. Arthur Draper. Art, what happened there when we came out with that funny prediction.

DRAPER: Well, we had a lot of troubles tonight. Strangely enough, they were all human and not the machine. When UNIVAC made it's first prediction, we just didn't believe it. So we asked UNIVAC to forget a lot of the trend information [concerning previous elections], assuming that it was wrong. . . . [but] as more votes came in, the odds came back, and it is now evident that we should have had nerve enough to believe the machine in the first place.

Draper's ordeal, which he described as "one of the worst evenings I ever spent in my life," created a field day for the news media. The headline over an editorial (November 11, 1952) in the *Journal* of Jacksonville, Florida, crowed: "Machine Makes a Monkey out of Man." In its issue of November 8, 1952, the *Washington Post* editorialized: "None of those stupid humans, including his inventors, would believe [UNIVAC] so they started jiggling . . . and ended by throwing the poor thing out of whack entirely, which seems to prove that those old fellows were right after all who said that only a hair's line of difference separates true genius from madness." CBS commentator Edward R. Murrow summed up the debacle tersely: "The trouble with machines is people."

With less than 7 percent of the vote tallied at 9:00 P.M. on election night, UNIVAC gave 438 electoral votes to Dwight D. Eisenhower and 93 to Adlai E. Stevenson. When the final count was in and the electoral college convened several weeks later, the official total was 442 for Eisenhower and 89 for Stevenson.

Many who had believed resolutely in the superiority of man's intellect now harbored doubts. A machine, a *computing* machine, had confounded the experts. And a new word, *UNIVAC*, which when uttered would conjure up fear, awe, or disdain, had become a prominent fixture in the American vocabulary.

CHAPTER 15

Breakout!

In 1950, while conceding that electronic computers were indeed stunning performers, no one in the know foresaw the need to build them in large numbers. True, a small specialized computer market might eventually develop, but for a company such as International Business Machines Corporation, which had built its prestige and profits on mechanical card calculators and tabulators, the amount of money to be made processing data electronically was considered negligible.

After all, had not most of the experts said so? Howard Aiken, for example, who had incorporated electronic circuits in his later models of the Mark series at Harvard University, was not alone in the belief that no more than six computers would ever be sold in the commercial marketplace. Multiply Aiken's estimate by two, or even three, and one ends up with the highly sanguine projection that perhaps twenty systems can fulfill all of the computing requirements of industry and government for the next decade or so. In the eyes of the powers-that-be at IBM, this was hardly the pot of gold at the end of the rainbow.

That viewpoint would soon change. The delivery of the first UNIVAC to the Bureau of the Census meant that, from Aiken's perspective, the number of future sales had been reduced to five. But soon after, Remington Rand won signed orders from the bureau for a second and a third UNIVAC. Unbelievable. Three electronic computers sold to just one agency of the federal government. Thomas Watson, Jr., then the newly installed president of IBM, recalls that when the Census Bureau ordered a third UNIVAC "we went into an absolute panic. Here was our traditional competitor, whom we always had been able to handle quite well, and now, before we knew it, it had five of these beasts installed—and we had none."

The unexpected spurt of orders that began flowing into Remington Rand headquarters in New York City, however, did not catch IBM completely off guard. There was a response waiting in the wings. Shortly after communist armies swarmed south across the 38th parallel into South Korea on June 25, 1950, Thomas Watson, Sr., dispatched a telegram to President Harry S. Truman. The resources of IBM, Watson told the president, are at the government's disposal. Watson's son, Tom Jr., was given the task of backing up his father's offer. The younger Watson, then an executive vice president of IBM, assigned an assistant, James Birkenstock, and Dr. Cuthbert C. Hurd, a former atomic scientist, to see what could be done. Birkenstock and Hurd went around the country visiting government laboratories and the research centers of major corporations doing business with the Defense Department and asked what they needed most. The answer they received nearly everywhere was "more computational power."

Birkenstock and Hurd came back to Watson with an alarming report. Their descriptions of the computing capacities needed for the government war work far exceeded, by several orders of magnitude, the processing speeds of the best machines IBM had to offer. But Birkenstock had an idea. He told Watson that IBM had the know-how—and the functional building blocks—to assemble an electronic computer that could perform the high-speed repetitive computations now hampering research in nuclear weaponry and aircraft and missile design. With Tom Jr.'s blessing, Birkenstock put a team of engineers to work and shortly after he went out to the government laboratories carrying blueprints of the proposed "IBM Defense Calculator."

It was an entirely new ball game. IBM had traditionally rented its tabulating machines for $300 or $400 per month. The estimated rental for the system Birkenstock was hawking, however, was $13,000 per month. The naysayers at IBM predicted that no one would pay that much, but they were wrong. Orders started coming in. Then, sensing that the name Defense Calculator was too limiting, IBM changed the identity of its new computer to "701," a designation more appropriate for the commercial marketplace. At IBM's manufacturing plant in Poughkeepsie, New York, general manager Smith Holmans told 701 production manager Richard Whalen to "lay out the department so it looks like a manufacturing set-up. It's the first one in the world. I can't tell you how to do it. But customers will be coming to visit us, so you've got to make it look like we know how to build computers."

As the first models of the 701 started taking shape in Poughkeepsie, Whalen, huddling with people in the controller's department, found that labor and material costs were running higher than anticipated. Obviously, the $13,-000 rental charge was too low. By this time Birkenstock had signed up nineteen customers, and parts for a nineteen-unit production run had already been ordered. Now, Birkenstock would have to go back and renegotiate contracts

The IBM 701, the first general-purpose commercial computer produced by International Business Machines Corporation.

charging 50 percent more, as high as $20,000 per month. But much to the surprise of the doubters at IBM, the original order total held firm; while there were some defections, others signed up to take their place. According to Thomas Watson, Jr., the success of the 701 "was enough to convince me we were in the electronics business and had better move fast. So we went from [a very few] to nearly five hundred electrical engineers in about two years. We would hire almost anyone who had an electronics background."

The first 701 off the production line in Poughkeepsie was shipped to the federal government's atomic weapons development center at Los Alamos, New Mexico, in March 1953. The following month, amid great fanfare, the 701 was formally introduced as a standard commercial product at a luncheon in New York City. Remington Rand, now no longer the only producer of general-purpose electronic computers, would have to cope with a competitor twice its size and one that could marshal what was then a staggering array of resources to achieve any goal it set for itself.

In the eight years since the end of World War II, IBM's revenues had quadrupled while Remington Rand's volume had doubled. Although not as impressive a performance as IBM's, it was a far better record than in the previous two decades. In the nearly twenty years following the spectacular amalgamation masterminded by James Rand in 1927, Remington Rand's growth was a disappointing 75 percent. Not even the stimulus of World War II would hasten its doddering pace. Sales in 1930 were $60 million; in 1946, $107 million. Rand's policy of scrimping on research and development, and thereby continuing to market products long after their time, may have stretched profits in the short term but was extremely damaging to his company's ability to compete in the long term. The legacy of this policy, reflected by a drop in Remington Rand's net worth from $43 million in 1930 to $30 million in 1946, would come back to haunt him as he girded to do battle with IBM in a tough new marketplace.

By the time IBM began delivering 701s in the spring of 1953, the company was already planning a successor machine, the 702. It was better and more powerful than its predecessor and would also make things more difficult for Remington Rand. However, the infant computer business was not the only turf upon which IBM and Remington Rand were competing. Most of the revenues and profits of both companies in the early 1950s came from the rental and sale of tabulating and punched-card machines. But IBM was dealing from a position of strength. Its indisputably larger customer base would be the springboard from which it would forge ahead to a far more commanding lead in computers in the years ahead. The 1954 financial statements of both companies are prophetic in this sense. On revenues of $244 million, Remington Rand earned $27 million in pretax profits, a return of 11 percent. But IBM, with revenues of $461 million, earned $165 million in pretax profits, a stunning 35 percent.

A breakthrough had run its course and was coming to an end. It had begun with ENIAC. Then EDVAC and BINAC.

And, of course, von Neumann's computer at the Institute for Advanced Study, which had spawned an impressive list of descendants: ORDVAC and ILLIAC, built at the University of Illinois; MANIAC (*Mathematical Analyzer Numerical Integrator and Counter*), which was the brainchild of Nicholas C. Metropolis at Los Alamos; and JOHNNIAC (in honor of "Johnny" von Neumann) at the Rand Corporation in Santa Monica, California.

Computer pioneers in Britain made significant contributions, too: EDSAC (*Electronic Delay Storage Automatic Calculator*); ACE (*Automatic Computing Engine*) at the National Physical Laboratory, Teddington; and MADM (*Manchester Automatic Digital Machine*) at Manchester.

The breakthrough was complete. The lone inventor in his workshop and the academic experimenters in university laboratories would give way to the supercharged, highly financed giant corporations. The mantle had been passed to a new breed. The breakout had begun.

Epilogue

In June 1946, when commenting on the plan to move ENIAC from the Moore School in Philadelphia to the Aberdeen Proving Ground in Maryland, Prof. Douglas R. Hartree warned that ENIAC should be handled "as if it were a bomb ready to go off." That advice was followed as well as it could be. But after the plan was implemented in late 1947, subsequent months were a nightmare for those who installed and operated ENIAC at Aberdeen.

Richard Clippinger, then the assistant director of the computation laboratory, recalls that "troubles occurred at such a high rate that it was impossible [to isolate them]." A mass attack appeared to be the only recourse. Tubes were pulled arbitrarily and replaced. Counters were disconnected at random and new ones put in their place. Finally, order was gradually restored. A study of the life expectancy of vacuum tubes revealed, surprisingly, that tubes were more prone to failure when new than old. This prompted the adoption of a tube-curing process. Before they were installed in ENIAC's circuits, all new tubes were put through a four- to six-hour "burn-in" on a test rack. This step weeded out the weak ones before they could be plugged into some isolated circuit and cause mischief later on.

When things were going well, and there were no emergencies to contend with, Homer Spence, a senior maintenance man who had been brought to Aberdeen from the Moore School, went around from one accumulator rack to another, tapping tubes and connecting joints with a small hammer. If a tube was a borderline case, there would be a flicker, and Spence would replace it.

Not every tube that performed erratically from time to time could be identified and replaced. However, Clippinger found a way to neutralize the effects of these intermittents on the firing and bombing tables that ENIAC produced during its long service: "Our bread and butter jobs on the ENIAC were the firing table computations, so I reprogrammed . . . so that we could compute one step to the next and then do it again and compare the results. If they were identical, we would accept them, and if they were not, we would do it a third time and look for two alike and repeat this until we got two alike, and then we would go on to the next."

Before Clippinger's remedy was applied, the mean failure rate was one every twenty to thirty seconds. Inasmuch as forty seconds of continuous computation were required to produce a single firing table, ENIAC was generating useful data only half the time it was operating. After his new method of computation was adopted, Clippinger found: "We'd get out hundreds of correct computations, and correct firing tables before we'd have one that forced us to do some maintenance work. . . . [Time] between errors jumped from twenty or thirty seconds up to [as much as] eight hours and [no less than] one hour. So the amount of work [completed] zoomed way up."

When power to its circuits was cut off for the last time on October 2, 1955, ENIAC had logged over 80,000 hours of metered computations. When it was dismantled in January 1956, parts of it were scavenged by collectors, and today its artifacts can be found in various institutions throughout the United States, including the U.S. Military Academy at West Point and the Smithsonian Institution in Washington, D.C.

After BINAC was crated and flown to Northrop's headquarters in Hawthorne, California, its fate became shrouded in controversy. There is only fragmentary evidence to support the contention that BINAC was ever used by Northrop. It remains the big question mark in the triumverate—ENIAC, BINAC, UNIVAC—when one looks at the record of early computing achievements. UNIVAC, on the other hand, has become something of a legend. From the day it went on-line in 1951 until its retirement in 1963, UNIVAC—Model-One-Number-One—labored more than 73,000 hours on the Census Bureau's demographic problems. In 1965, nearly seventeen years after the first model was delivered to the Census Bureau, six UNIVAC I systems were still operating effectively. The last remaining unit in that historic series was dismantled in 1970.

Bibliography

Alt, Franz L. "Archaeology of Computers—Reminiscences 1945–47." *Communications of the ACM*, vol. 15, no. 7 (July 1972).

Babbage, Charles. *Passages from the Life of a Philosopher*. London, 1864.

Bernstein, Jeremy. *The Analytical Engine* New York: Random House, 1963.

Bush, Vannevar. *Pieces of the Action*. New York: Morrow, 1970.

Costello, John. "The Little Known Creators of the Computer." *Nation's Business*, vol. 59, no. 12 (1971).

Darby, Edwin. "A. C. Nielsen Gets the Facts." *Commerce* (December 1978).

Davis, Nuel Pharr. *Lawrence & Oppenheimer*. New York: Simon & Schuster, 1968.

Evans, Christopher. *The Micro Millennium*. New York: Viking, 1979.

Goldstine, H. H. *The Computer from Pascal to Von Neumann*. Princeton, N.J.: Princeton University Press, 1972.

Hartree, D. R. "The ENIAC, An Electronic Computing Machine." *Nature*, vol. 158, no. 4015 (October 12, 1946).

Lukoff, Herman. *From Dits to Bits: A Personal History of the Electronic Computer*. Portland, Oreg.: Robotics Press, 1979.

Malik, Rex. *And Tomorrow the World? Inside IBM*. London: Millington, Ltd., 1975.

McCorduck, Pamela. *The Machine Who Thinks.* San Francisco: W. H. Freeman & Co., 1979.

Oppenheimer, J. Robert. *Letters and Recollections.* Edited by Alice Kimball Smith and Charles Weiner. Cambridge, Mass.: Harvard University Press, 1980.

Sprague, R. E. "A Western View of Computer History." *Communications of the ACM* (July 1972).

Stibitz, George. "The Relay Computers at Bell Labs." *DATAMATION* (April 1967).

Tropp, Henry C. "The Effervescent Years: A Retrospective." *Spectrum* (February 1974).

Index

183